Also by Bruce Pandolfini:
Let's Play Chess
Bobby Fischer's Outrageous Chess Moves
One Move Chess by the Champions

Principles of the New Chess

Superb New Techniques
Developed in the USSR
and the USA

by
Bruce Pandolfini

A FIRESIDE BOOK
Published by Simon & Schuster Inc.
New York   London   Toronto   Sydney   Tokyo   Singapore

To all my students
for all they've taught me

Copyright © 1986 by Bruce Pandolfini

A Fireside Book
Published by Simon & Schuster, Inc.
Simon & Schuster Building
Rockefeller Center
1230 Avenue of the Americas
New York, New York 10020

FIRESIDE and colophon are registered trademarks of Simon & Schuster, Inc.

Designed by Stanley S. Drate/Folio Graphics Co., Inc.

Manufactured in the United States of America

10 9 8 7 6 5 4

Library of Congress Cataloging in Publication Data

Pandolfini, Bruce.
  Principles of the new chess.

  "A Fireside book."
  Includes index.
  1. Chess. I. Title.
GV1445.P258   1986   794.1'2   85-23387

ISBN: 0-671-60719-7

Acknowledgments

Editorially, I would like to thank Idelle Pandolfini, Carol Ann Caronia, Deborah Bergman, and Roane Carey. Chessically, thanks to grandmaster Lev Alburt and masters Bruce Alberston, Douglas Bellizzi, David Daniels, Mark Dvoretsky, Larry D. Evans, Svetozar Jovanovic, George Kane, Matthew Looks, Sekhar Sahu, Larry Tamarkin, Frank Thornally, and Sunil Weeramantry.

Contents

II
Middle Game

III
Endgame: Just a Little

Introduction

The New Chess is really a new way of teaching—and learning—a very old game.

In the United States the modern science of chess teaching took off back in 1972 with the spectacular Fischer-Spassky world championship "match of the century" in Reykjavik, Iceland. Millions observed, move by move, via television, the progress of this explosive contest from opening to middlegame to endgame. For many it was a proper introduction to what chess is all about, and it undoubtedly opened the eyes of chess teachers dissatisfied with the usual musty teaching methods.

U.S. chess instruction before 1972 had been casual and undisciplined, with a few notable exceptions. It often consisted of nothing more than game playing, with the better player summarily commenting at the end. Some teachers did attempt to follow a curriculum, usually based on a classic textbook. Often these books were written by brilliant players with a tremendous natural grasp of the game's essentials who delivered instructional systems inspired by mathematics and science. Such systems were complete, logical, and intellectually satisfying in their abstract perfection.

Unfortunately, these generalized approaches were unsuccessful with many students. The masters who devised them, however ingeniously, never really had enough teaching experience to test out their ideas on students. They related to people who already knew something about chess, not beginners. Most of the instructors, themselves so far removed from the elementary level, had neither affinity nor much sympathy for a newcomer's dilemma.

In the 1970s, American teachers, myself included, began to incorporate more dynamic ideas into instruction. Perhaps this development was influenced in a way by teachers in the Soviet Union who had already done just that. Though the method presented here is my own, it was corroborated and commended by my Russian counterparts who are doing many of the same things.

Old vs. New

A basic tenet of the old methods had been that one should first learn the endgame, the third and final stage of a chess game. This method stressed goal orientation, for the last stage was necessarily closer to the end of the game. Fewer pieces were on the board, so it was easier to analyze. The basic mates (for example, King and two Bishops versus a lone King) show the powers of the pieces unobscured by complicating forces or circumstances. Moreover, teachers felt that since the basic mates they used as examples (or related ones) occur often, chess students should be very familiar with them.

I initially accepted these premises, along with many other young teachers of the 1970s. And, in an unprecedented number of cases, we were actually able to put these concepts to the test. (I myself have since given over 15,000 private lessons.)

The results were staggering. A high percentage of chess teachers found they had to modify the classic methods if they were to retain their students' interest. The traditional methods worked for some novices, but a far greater number of students found the standard techniques stale and obsolete. There were simply too many obvious contradictions and problems. A more creative and exciting approach was needed.

The goal of chess is checkmate, which is a logical outcome of inspired opening play and middlegame mating patterns. But the endgame gives little hint of the earlier phases, focusing mainly on the nuances of pawn promotion. Because there are fewer pieces on the board, endgames require very precise calculation well beyond the scope of most beginners. Masters are excited by endgames, but newcomers generally find them dull. Without the preceding phases the endgame can seem to the untrained eye as diverse as the universe itself. In the opening and middlegame, the presence of other pieces actually assists classification, whereas the board's relative emptiness in the endgame provides few signposts to direct thinking. Beginners prefer—and require—a more total approach to chess that includes the opening and middlegame. The concepts in these phases are fairly easy to comprehend and remember.

To understand the powers of the pieces, it's sensible to see them in relation to other forces by studying the tactics of the opening and middlegame. The basic mates of the endgame, on the other hand, offer little information—the totality of the game is simply not there for beginners. Anyway, as many vociferously complain, they hardly ever even get into endgames. They usually lose in the opening or middlegame, long before most true endgames can develop. The ability to convert an extra pawn into a win (a basic endgame plan) doesn't really prevent getting checkmated in twenty moves.

No wonder many students have felt some distaste for the traditional approach to chess. Lessons should induce players to enjoy the challenge and stimulation of a good game. Too much endgame analysis is stultifying.

The lure of chess lies in variety. Beginning at the beginning will help most students realize the game's immense possibilities. And proceeding sequentially and laterally—i.e. evaluating several lines of thought at once—across the phases reveals the game's richness.

This is what the New Chess is all about—the vibrant, imaginative, and varied approaches developed by the present generation of chess teachers around the country and the world. Each one has found original solutions to old problems, and together they have advanced the evolution of the game as never before.

My Method

In my own teaching, I tend to use the same method, though no two of my lessons have ever been the same. The modus operandi is a mock encounter in which the student and I act out a game in progress. The moves serve as branching points for discussion. They generate information about the student's play and enable me to interject timely principles, concepts, and advice. The interaction of a real chess game is simulated throughout.

The lesson must be natural. The game goes wherever the student's needs and interests take it. Discussions focus on immediately relevant questions, and everything is fashioned so that it applies to the situation at hand. The complete picture is significant. A concept's limitations are as important as the concept itself, and so most ideas are given full play. I stress understanding, not memory. The reasoning process is dissected. How a problem is solved may take precedence over the actual solution.

The emphasis is on spontaneity tempered by relevance. I try to work with the student's strengths and propensities, though I never exclude an appropriate idea, even if it's beyond his present scope. Students need to be challenged, and it would serve no purpose to skip over something that's truly germane. To do so might even frustrate the learning process.

When opportune, I try to use lateral thinking. I'm not afraid to improvise apparently unrelated principles and positions if indirectly they reinforce a point. Nor are concepts from other disciplines beyond the boundaries of my lessons either, especially if they make the chess more lucid. I want to help the student as the game's mysteries unfold—I want to give him knowledge and joy—and to these ends I will implement whatever seems to work.

This book is a synthesis of my typical private lessons, using an instructional game developed interactively by myself and students from the United States and Russia. Abundant introductory principles can be found here, along with supplementary examples and advice from teachers around the world. Many of my techniques were confirmed by Soviet teachers as part of their arsenal.

Other ideas stem from the new wave of American educators now leaving their marks on the next generation of masters. But perhaps the most significant contributions come from the many students who invested so much time in learning how to appreciate and play a better game of chess. They taught me much of what I know, and now, through *The Principles of the New Chess,* I trust they can teach you.

Before You Start

Running throughout is an instructional game—the connective tissue for every idea in the book—which was the basis for a few private sessions I gave in the fall of 1984 in the USSR and later in the United States. The moves of the game were jointly conceived by myself and Russian and American students. All the didactic material—my principles, concepts, techniques, advice, examples, and so on—was integrated into the course of the game. The questions posed, and the answers, are comparable to those in the actual lessons.

The course is designed mainly for students who have not studied formally but know how the pieces move. Rank beginners can follow it after they've learned the rules, and more experienced amateurs might sift it for reinforcement and clarification. Teachers also may find some suggestions helpful in their own lessons, as was the case with my Soviet counterparts. Presented here, in both word and symbol, as I teach them, are the fundamentals and principles of the New Chess.

Algebraic Notation

The best way to read this book is while sitting at a chessboard on the White side, with the pieces in their starting positions. Most of the material can be understood without playing out the moves, by either reading the descriptive comments or examining the helpful diagrams accompanying the text. But you will derive greater benefit if you learn the simplified algebraic notation offered here. The system works as follows:

- The board is regarded as an eight-by-eight graph with sixty-four squares in all.
- The *files* (the rows of squares going up the board) are lettered a through h, beginning from White's left.
- The *ranks* (the rows of squares going across the board) are numbered 1 through 8, beginning from White's nearest row.

You can therefore identify any square by combining a letter and a number, with the letter written first (see diagram A). For example, the square on which White's King stands in the original position is e1, while the original square for Black's King is e8. All squares are always named from White's point of view.

Symbols You Should Know

K means King
Q means Queen
R means Rook
B means Bishop
N means Knight

Pawns are not symbolized when recording the moves. But if referred to in discussions, they are named by the letter of the file occupied—the pawn on the b-file is the b-pawn. If a pawn makes a capture, one merely indicates the file the capturing pawn starts on. Thus, if a White pawn on b2 captures a Black pawn, Knight, Bishop, Rook, or Queen on a3, it is written **bxa3.** In indicating a capture, name the square captured, not the enemy unit.

x means captures
+ means check
0-0 means castles Kingside
0-0-0 means castles Queenside
! means good move

‼ means very good move
? means questionable move
?? means blunder
1. means White's first move
1... means Black's first move (when appearing independently of White's)
(1–0) means White wins
(0–1) means Black wins

Reading the Line Score of a Game

Consider diagram B. White could mate in three moves and it would be written this way:

1. Nc7+ Kb8 2. Na6+ Ka8 3. Bc6 mate.

1. Nc7+ means that White's first move was Knight moves to c7 giving check.
Kb8 means that Black's first move was King to b8.
2. Na6+ means that White's second move was Knight to a6 check.
Ka8 means that Black's second move was King to a8.
3. Bc6 mate means that White's third move was Bishop to c6 giving mate.

Note that the number of the move is written only once, appearing just before White's play. In this book, the actual moves are given in **boldface** type and are marked with this symbol (【♟】), as are the diagrams that depict them. The analyzed alternatives appear in regular type.

DIAGRAM A

DIAGRAM B

The Basics

All Chess Is Divided into Three Parts

An ordinary chess game lasts about forty moves and has three phases:

- The opening
- The middlegame
- The endgame

There are no hard-and-fast boundary lines between the parts; the transitions are subtle and may be difficult to perceive and appreciate. The *opening*, usually lasting from ten to fifteen moves, is the building foundation on which the forces are gathered and prepared for action. The *middlegame* is more concerned with planning and strategy—pieces are maneuvered and repositioned to achieve the opening's objectives. In the *endgame,* the stronger side tries to capitalize on its accumulated advantages while the weaker side tries to offset its weaknesses.

White's Supreme Advantage

It's advantageous to go first, to get in the first blow. It's much harder to defend against an opponent's determined course of action. (The only time this isn't so in chess is when you are in *zugzwang,* a German word signifying situations in which having to move is undesirable. But *zugzwang* is primarily an endgame concept and has little currency in the opening.)

Thus White starts the game with a natural *initiative.* A chessplayer is said to have the initiative when he can force the action and direct the flow of play. This gives you an advantage in *time,* which is one of the five main elements of chess (the other four being space, material, pawn structure, and King safety).

White will try to maintain this temporal advantage until able to convert it into something concrete, by winning material or forcing checkmate. Black (the defender) meanwhile must try to squelch the onslaught and then seize the initiative with a timely counterattack.

The attacker (White from the opening position) can sometimes err and still not lose because the defender may be mentally unprepared to launch a counteroffensive on a moment's notice. A mistake by the defender, on the other hand, is more likely to be fatal. This is so because the attacker is more attuned to the possibility of such lapses—he's already factored them into his plans. The attacker generally knows what he's trying to do ahead of time, whereas the defender isn't quite as sure until it happens. It's easier to act than react. A player who ignores the initiative is like a boxer who allows his opponent a free swing. To paraphrase some lines from Shakespeare: "Twice armed is he who knows his cause is just, but thrice armed is he who gets his blow in fust."

Using the initiative, White should strive for two fundamental aims out of the opening:

• To develop his forces
• To play for the center

Development

A fundamental aim of the opening is mobilization of your forces for action. You should *develop* them, which means increasing their scope and power. You do this by moving a few pawns out of the way and then transferring the pieces on the back rank from their original squares to more useful ones, especially toward the center. (Chess terminology distinguishes between *pawns*—the units occupying each player's second rank at the start—and *pieces*—Kings, Queens, Rooks, Bishops, and Knights. Every kind of chessman is called a piece except for the pawn.)

You have a better chance of accomplishing your aims if you attack with all your pieces, not just one or two. A rule of thumb is to develop a different piece on each move so that you build a juggernaut assault with numerous forces. Don't attack aimlessly with the same pieces (especially your Queen). Such sporadic sorties should be easily repulsed by a circumspect opponent's coordinated forces.

Once fully mobilized or developed, you can strike with authority as necessary. On the other hand, don't develop merely for development's sake. Aim to develop and threaten at the same time. This will limit your opponent's freedom of action, for, in responding to your threats, he will be hindered in bringing his men to their ideal squares.

Threats

A *threat* is an attempt to gain advantage, generally by inflicting some immediate harm on the enemy position. Most commonly a threat is designed to win material, either by capturing for nothing or by surrendering less force than you gain (giving up a pawn to capture a Knight, which is worth three pawns, etc.). More serious threats involve the King, while less important ones may hinge on dominating certain squares or creating weaknesses in your opponent's fortress.

You cannot ignore threats. You've got to defend against them, produce a more immediate or serious threat of your own, or respond with a simultanous defense and attack. The latter is usually best, as it affords an opportunity to seize the initiative.

One contribution of the Soviets is to play the Black side of the opening phase very sharply, so that every move is fraught with threats and tension. This has constrained serious international competitors, such as the U.S.'s own Bobby Fischer, to subject the opening moves to extremely deep analysis, which has enriched the theory of the game immeasurably.

Controlling the Center

The most important squares on the chessboard are in the center. The *center* is the portion of the board consisting of the squares d4, d5, e4, and e5, as outlined in diagram 1 below. In many discussions, the central region is augmented to include the squares immediately surrounding the center: c3, c4, c5, c6, d6, e6, f6, f5, f4, f3, e3, and d3. This expanded area is known as the *enlarged* or *big center* and is also represented in diagram 1. Pieces sitting on these squares generally enjoy greater mobility, which means they have more possible moves and greater flexibility.

DIAGRAM 1

This region is the key to the shifting fortunes of battle. A piece stationed there, on a relatively clear board, can usually move in any direction with little trouble. Such a piece has greater *mobility* and *options,* meaning it has potential access to more squares.

Pieces away from the center enjoy less mobility and *influence* less space (the general term for an advantage in overall control of squares). Pieces placed near the edge of the board usually aren't as flexible. Even if the center isn't totally blocked or guarded, just try to maneuver an out-of-the-way piece from side to side when suddenly you have to. Only the Rook can be as mobile on the wing as in the center. On an empty board, it can move to any of fourteen different squares no matter where it's placed. Every other piece, including the King, is more powerful from a central post.

To test out some of the assertions made here, place each piece in turn on various squares in the center and on the wings of an otherwise empty chessboard. As the following chart illustrates, the center is the place to be.

PIECE	Squares It Can Move to When on				Total Mobility*
	e4	f6	b2	h1	from All Squares
QUEEN	27	25	23	21	1456
ROOK	14	14	14	14	896
BISHOP	13	11	9	7	560
KNIGHT	8	8	3	2	336
KING	8	8	8	3	420

*Total numbers of squares a piece can move to from all the squares on the board added together.

By controlling the center you might be able to drive a wedge into the enemy's position, splitting the opposing army in two. You thereby prevent your opponent from coordinating or pulling together his forces effectively. Lack of free and easy movement and its resulting options should cause your adversary plenty of problems.

• Guard the center.
• Occupy it.
• Influence it.

How to accomplish these tasks, and further reasons for doing so, will be explored later.

1

The Opening

White's First Move

What's a Good First Move?

 I recommend that most players begin with **1. e4**.

DIAGRAM 2

There are a number of reasons for this beginning. For one, it places a pawn right in the center, immediately staking White's claim to the sector. In addition to the key central square d5, White zeroes in on another salient point, f5 (a Knight positioned here can often inflict great damage if Black is castled Kingside). The thrust **1. e4** contributes powerfully to development, for White can now bring out his Queen and light-square Bishop. Advancing the e-pawn has opened diagonals for both of them. Finally, this central stab is an aggressive act.

Far less imposing would be 1. e3, a push for only one square. It would open diagonals for the same two pieces, but it wouldn't seriously pressure the center. Too, by going only one square, White places another obstacle before the dark-square Bishop, which now cannot come out as easily. Generally, moving a central pawn only one square on the first move for White is ill-grounded. A seasoned opponent will view this as inexperience or cowardice and may be able to exploit the information at a critical moment.

Going two squares instead of one also seizes more space. Usually, the more advanced your pawns, the more space or room you have behind the lines. When we get further into our lesson, we shall see that the placement of pawns is paramount to the subsequent course of the game.

Another reason I recommend the King-pawn opening of **1. e4** is that it tends to produce positions that are more open, direct, and less confusing. Less complicated situations are easier to evaluate. Blocked positions, especially those with interlocked central pawns, are ordinarily more subtle. They'll be dealt with somewhat later, in line with a student's more advanced development.

What would a Soviet teacher do if his student played the opening passively (1. e3)? He would compel him to do the opposite as often as possible. To overcome the fear of being aggressive, the student would be coached to play the sharpest opening lines every chance he gets. The idea is to bombard a problem until it becomes commonplace and ceases to be a problem. For a while, it may result in losing games, but eventually, from experience, you will be more able to cope with the unfamiliar. It may even become a steadfast weapon.

Isn't a Queen-pawn opening also good?

Yes, but it's generally more sophisticated. The advance 1. d4 attacks and occupies a central square (e5 and d4 respectively). It enables the Queen to enter the fray too, but not via a diagonal as with **1. e4.** Here it must escape through the d-file. Moreover, rather than the light-square Bishop, it's White's dark-square

Bishop that can develop. The Queen offers ready-made support for the d-pawn's advance—that's an advantage. The e-pawn, on the other hand, sits in the center without initial backup.

Nevertheless, for reasons not yet clear, 1. d4 will more likely produce a slower, obstacle-ridden game that can manufacture real problems for a novice. Though 1. d4 and **1. e4** are relatively as strong, it makes more sense for newcomers to begin with the latter.

What other good first moves does White have?

There are several plausible first moves in addition to moving either center pawn two squares. They include 1. Nf3, 1. g3, 1. c4, and 1. b3. But to play them intelligently and to understand how they can be used winningly requires a much more informed approach than most newcomers have. Such moves as 1. a3, 1. b4, 1. f4, and 1. Nc3 have also been essayed successfully. Even a risky spike such as 1. g4 can't be ignored. Yet none of these moves, both reasonable and unreasonable, offers as much for the novitiate as 1. e4 or 1. d4.

If after playing 1. e4 you were allowed to make a second move before Black responds, what should you play?

Though quite a number of moves would be useful here, the one that makes the most sense is 2. d4. After that, of the four squares in the center, White occupies two and controls the other

DIAGRAM 3

two. The Queen's scope would also increase and the dark-square Bishop could then be developed too. This formation is called a *classical* or *ideal pawn center.* It's classical because the concept goes back to the earliest generations of strong masters. It's ideal because White can now practically undertake any reasonable course of action.

Black will have a difficult time, for he will not be able to fight back adequately in the central region and may fall behind in development. He also faces having his forces driven back by the menacing White pawns, making it even harder for his pieces to find good squares.

How does this help White's development?

Remarkably, White is now ready to develop all his pieces without having to move another pawn! In fact, White needs only eight moves at most to mobilize his forces from here. He could move his Knights to f3 and c3, his Bishops to c4 and f4, and his Queen to d3. He could castle Kingside (0-0), and finally move his Rooks to the central files by putting his King Rook on e1 and his Queen Rook on d1, as in diagram 4.

DIAGRAM 4

White's moves were 1. e4 2. d4 3. Nf3 4. Nc3 5. Bc4 6. Bf4 7. Qd3 8. 0-0 9. Rf-e1 10. Ra-d1. These ten moves together form an opening scheme. *Opening schemes* are defined by the placement of the pieces around a particular pawn structure. Diagram 5 shows an alternative scheme from the same pawn advances.

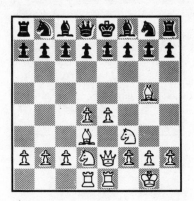

DIAGRAM 5

White's moves here were 1. e4 2. d4 3. Nf3 4. Bd3 5. 0-0 6. Bg5 7. Nb-d2 8. Qe2 9. Rf-e1 10. Ra-d1. Of course there are other ways to develop the pieces around this pawn center. This is a model situation, where Black hasn't had an opportunity to respond to White's moves. In a real game, White would have to reply to Black's moves and plans. White's play would be more in a state of flux.

For the purpose of these exercises, as well as in actual chess games, the King is said to be developed when it is safely castled, and the Rooks are *mobilized* when they can stand sentinel over the central files from e1 and d1. Later on we will have more to say about the movement of the King and Rooks and also the significance of castling.

Can the position of the pieces in diagram 4 be achieved with one less move?

Practically, yes. A move can be saved if White castles Queen-side instead of Kingside. On move eight for example, White could continue with 8. 0-0-0 and 9. Rh-e1. Except for the King, the rest of the White pieces are on the same squares. The main difference here is that the White King winds up on the Queenside.

DIAGRAM 6

Therefore, is castling Queenside preferable to castling Kingside?

No, though everything depends on the circumstances you're presented with in an actual game. Kingside castling occurs more often mainly because it can happen sooner, since there are fewer pieces to get out of the way. It might be better to position the King on a particular side, depending on the game's development. This is true throughout for all aspects of play.

- Don't ignore your opponent's moves.
- Everything you do should be influenced by what he or she does.

If given three unanswered moves to start a game, should you move a third pawn after 1. e4 and 2. d4?

If you did, you could still come away with an overwhelming position, as after 1. e4 2. d4 3. c4 (diagram 7).

But a third pawn move is not necessary. As already indicated, you need only move the two center pawns to develop all your pieces. Rather than move a third pawn, it is better to commence the mobilization of the pieces on the back rank. You've laid down the front lines (the e-pawn and the d-pawn); now bring up the support troops behind them.

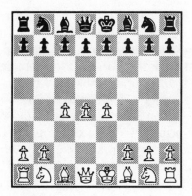

DIAGRAM 7

Since you never get three free moves at the start, why bother considering it?

In many cases your opponent plays totally irrelevant moves that have no bearing on what's really happening. If so, you will actually be able to develop as if he's playing no moves at all. Then you will want to proceed optimally, aiming for the ideal setup. This would be if your opponent were first to present moves like 1...a6 2...a5 and 3...h5. Then you could more or less do whatever you want, as if he didn't exist.

One Soviet technique is to have beginners play as many unanswered moves from the start as they wish, until they've achieved the perfect position. The only proviso is that nothing can be moved beyond the fourth rank. The exercise helps the student think in terms of schemes, plans, and goals. It certainly clues one in on the student's imagination, and also indexes his propensity for problem solving. Beyond this, the technique heightens awareness, while transforming the student into an active participant rather than a passive listener. In trying this, I've often directed the student to definite goals by integrating leading questions at key instants, such as "What is the weakest point in Black's original position?" This is designed to make the student focus on the square f7, which initially is defended solely by the Black King.

Since moving both center pawns two squares each is what White would do under ideal conditions, then this is what he should be striving for in actual play. But real opponents will not sit back and let him proceed without contention. They'll try to make this plan difficult or undesirable for White to execute. That's what chess is, a struggle for control, as was emphasized by former world champion Emanuel Lasker (1868-1941) in his play and writings (he actually wrote a philosophical treatise entitled *Struggle,* which drew analogies from chess). White is trying to convert his first move advantage into a win, and Black will try to offset that advantage and steal the initiative. The better idea and follow-up plan wins. Two opening principles emerge from this discussion:

• Try to move both center pawns two squares each.
• Don't move too many pawns, especially in the opening.

Consequences of Bad Pawn Moves

We've suggested that unnecessary pawn moves waste time that could be put to better use developing pieces. Especially in the opening, every *tempo* (as in music, a unit of time—a move) is critical and should be utilized for the mobilization of the forces.

Unwise pawn moves also create weaknesses. Once pawns advance beyond a point, they can never again guard the squares they've passed. Unlike pieces, pawns can't move backward. Their consequences are irreversible. If you make a bad pawn move, you're stuck with it. With pieces, sometimes you get an opportunity to retract errors at the cost of a wasted move (though that can mean trouble too).

Actually, since pawns are more expendable (less valuable) than other chessmen, they are the best defenders of squares. Every enemy piece must respect a square guarded by a pawn, for if the piece lands on that square, it may be captured, resulting in the loss of material.

Pawns are particularly good defenders for the King, where their intact arrangement around a castled King's position tends to ward off most enemy invaders. Move those pawns, and you might expose your King to an onslaught. Once those squares are made accessible to enemy forces, the game could be as good as over.

Again, don't move pawns unnecessarily. Only move pawns when it is clearly helpful or required by the position. For example, unless you have a good reason for doing otherwise and really understand the implications, try not to move your Rook-pawns in the opening. Some of the shortest games in chess history have resulted from a violation of this general rule.

Even deadlier consequences may result from pushing the King Bishop-pawn (the f-pawn), for it greatly weakens the uncastled King's position. (This is a far less serious offense—moving the f-pawn—when the King is already castled Kingside, and indeed the King Rook may be able to capitalize on the opening of the f-file.)

Among the numerous examples of bad pawn play in the opening are the following short games:

1. f3?

A horrible move that develops nothing and opens the gateway to White's King.

1...e5

An excellent move that attacks the center, while clearing the hatch for the Queen and dark-square Bishop.

2. g4??

A blunder that loses immediately.

2...Qh4 mate.

White moved the only two pawns that could expose his King in this manner. Note the g-pawn can't move backward to block the Queen's check (diagram 8).

Curiously, White needs an extra move to do the same to Black, which illustrates that quick games aren't won, they're lost, usually by bad pawn moves. Five-year-old Robert LeDonne of New Jersey mated CBS reporter Tony Hernandez at the Marshall Chess Club in 1973 thusly: 1. e4 f6? 2. d4 g5?? 3. Qh5 mate.

Even masters are prone to these mistakes, as shown in a game between two French masters in the 1920s (diagram 9). It went:

DIAGRAM 8

DIAGRAM 9

1. d4 Nf6

Black's move prevents White from building a classical pawn center by moving his e-pawn two squares. It also develops a piece toward the center.

2. Nd2?

A developing move, but one that at least temporarily blocks in the Queen and dark-square Bishop.

2...e5!?

A somewhat audacious attempt to commandeer the initiative by a temporary sacrifice of a pawn.

3. dxe5 Ng4 4. h3??

White's nudging pawn move is totally gratuitous, unnecessary, and blunderous.

4...Ne3!!

And White resigned. Either he must allow his Queen to be taken by the Knight, or capture the Knight, exposing his King to a deadly check from the Queen. Thus if 5. fxe3, White is bereft of pawn protection for the square g3, so that 5...Qh4+ mates next (if 6. g3, then 6...Qxg3 mate). The culprit was the thrust 4. h3??, which left g3 less defended and vulnerable.

Black's First Move

 Black (as per diagram 10) answers White's **1. e4** with **1...e5**.

DIAGRAM 10

So far this opening falls into the double King-pawn variety, meaning that both sides have advanced their King pawns two squares each. Surely Black does this for reasons similar to White's, but with a profound difference. Black's thrust is additionally concerned with dissuading White's eventual d4. Black is thinking defense. White, in turn, is not really thinking of stopping Black's d5 (though such an advance could be important for Black down the road). White's got the initiative and will strike first. In a sense, he's playing for a win and Black's playing for a draw—with the same move!

Should Black Try to Copy White's Play?

Absolutely not. Even in the present case, one can have different motives for assuming the same position. Anyway, for practical reasons it's inevitably impossible to copy for very long. If one side gives a check, for example, his opponent must first get out of check before he can follow suit. It may be impossible to restore the same setup as the first player after that. And suppose the first player gives checkmate? There's no last licks in chess—the game's over.

In addition to these obvious drawbacks there may be more subtle reasons preventing symmetrical play. The Petrov Defense provides a clear instance. After 1. e4 e5 2. Nf3 Nf6 the Petrov is established.

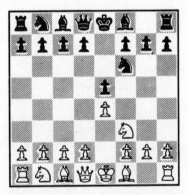

DIAGRAM 11

If White now captured the e-pawn 3. Nxe5, it would be a mistake for Black to continue 3...Nxe4. Before capturing this pawn, he must first play 3...d6 to drive back the White Knight. If he errs with 3...Nxe4, he runs into a pickle by 4. Qe2, when 4...Qe7 fails to 5. Qxe4, defending his own Knight from capture by Black's Queen. And if Black retreats his Knight after 4. Qe2 (4...Nf6—See diagram 12), then 5. Nc6+, a discovered attack to the enemy King and a direct assault on the opposing Queen wins a lot of material.

DIAGRAM 12

To the untrained eye, it may seem that masters occasionally do play the same or similar moves (more often the latter.) If so, they almost always do so for at least slightly different reasons, and they remain vigilant for possibilities to break the symmetry favorably, increasing or expropriating the initiative in the process. Bobby Fischer, in particular, is a genius at finding egress in apparently symmetrical games.

This Reminds Me ...

I recall three problems with humorous solutions that require each side to play the same first three moves, so that on the fourth move White gives mate:

A) 1. c4 c5 2. Qa4 Qa5 3. Qc6 Qc3 4. Qxc8 mate.

DIAGRAM 13

B) 1. d4 d5 2. Qd3 Qd6 3. Qf5 Qf4 4. Qxc8 mate.

C) 1. d4 d5 2. Qd3 Qd6 3. Qh3 Qh6 4. Qxc8 mate.

DIAGRAM 14

No, we didn't say these were good moves, just amusing ones. Note the last two examples result in the same final mating position, represented by diagram 14. If you're playing a stronger player, don't think you can equalize by imitating his moves against himself. It just doesn't work that way.

Again to our game: Has Black any other moves to dissuade White from playing 2. d4?

Black (in diagram 2) has several alternatives to **1...e5** that stop a favorable 2. d4. For one, he can play the Sicilian Defense, 1...c5, which, like 1...e5, immediately observes the square d4. In both cases, White's advance 2. d4 could then be answered by a pawn capture. Less effective would be 1...Nc6 for stopping 2. d4 (though Black's move wouldn't be bad if he followed with a different but consistent plan), because Black couldn't safely capture the d-pawn (his Knight would be taken by White's Queen).

An alternative approach would be not to guard against 2. d4, but to challenge the White e-pawn. Thus after 1...Nf6, Alekhine's Defense, White would lose his e-pawn if he continued 2. d4. The same is true of 1...d5, the Center Counter, though this is less desirable for it encourages the newcomer to bring out the Queen early, which as we shall soon see, is a no-no. All these moves (c5, Nc6, Nf6, and d5) are possible for Black, as well as several others, but they require a more developed understanding of chess to play correctly. In terms of a beginner's less mature understanding, **1...e5** is the most direct way to cope with the potential of 2. d4.

Can White safely play 2. d4?

DIAGRAM 15

He certainly can, without losing material, for if 2...exd4, he can recoup his pawn by 3.Qxd4. So 2. d4 doesn't lose a pawn as many newcomers are initially apt to think. Nor is it a bad strategy to trade White's d-pawn for Black's e-pawn. White is not playing d4 solely with the idea of establishing a classical pawn center but rather to open the game for his pieces to come out. (Don't mistakenly reason that you shouldn't play d4 if you can't maintain your d-pawn.) Newcomers sometimes fear that trading material is the same as losing material. It's just not so:

• You win material if you get more than you give up.
• You lose material if you get less than you give up.
• You trade material if you get the same in value as you give up.

Winning material is generally good, losing material is generally bad, and trading material is not generally either one, but dependent on the requirements of a given position. If it turns out to be a bad transaction, it will be for non-material reasons. And by necessity, if a trade is desirable for one player it tends to be disagreeable for the other.

Then, is 2. d4 a good move?

It's still not that simple. No matter how White plays, it reveals his intentions a little prematurely, though it does not lead to a losing game. The main problem is that after 2...exd4 (diagram 16), White might be tempted to reestablish material equality by taking back the pawn with his Queen, 3. Qxd4 (diagram 17)

DIAGRAM 16

DIAGRAM 17

Is It Bad to Bring out the Queen Early?

Generally, yes. The Queen's power is almost mind-boggling. But even so, it's vulnerable. Every time the other side attacks it, it likely has to move away. The result could be a waste of time and the initiative falling into the opponent's hands. If he uses these attacks to build his own game by getting out new pieces, he will be developing at your expense.

Notice, for example, Black can attack a White Queen standing on the square h5 by playing his King Knight from its original square (g8) to the fine post (f6). Because the Queen is worth so much in comparison to the Knight, it's virtually compelled to retreat (White might elect to defend his Queen instead if it were of the same or less value as the Knight), probably with nothing gained. Likely it would lose the initiative and the advantage of the first move. Attacks with just one or two pieces, even if one of them is the powerful Queen, seldom work early in the game against experienced opponents (they shouldn't work against anyone). Skilled defenders will easily parry your threats and strike back with fierce, and often devastating, counterthrusts.

After 1. e4 e5 2. d4 exd4 3. Qxd4, doesn't White's Queen stand powerfully in the center?

Not really. The problem is that Black can now play 3...Nc6, developing a new piece toward the center and attacking the White Queen simultaneously. White will have to move his Queen to safety, losing a move, and allowing the initiative to pass into Black's hands. It's Black who is here directing the flow of play.

DIAGRAM 18

Back Up the Queen

If you bring out the queen early, have a very good reason for doing so. Try to attack in number, using all your pieces, especially the minor ones (Bishops and Knights). Don't attack impetuously with lean forces.

Prepare the Queen's entrance by bringing out the support troops first. Eventually the Queen will be ready for action, and then it can become a real menace to weak points in the enemy's camp because of its wide range and striking power. Since it's able to attack in all directions, it's capable of delivering multiple threats with the same move, which is the main way to win material advantages.

The Queen she's a wondrous piece . . .

Newcomers naturally overuse the Queen because they are impressed by its great powers. How it got this way is mysterious. Originally it was a weak piece, moving one diagonal square at a time, like an inferior Bishop. Its rising importance in chess seems to have paralleled the expanding role of ruling queens in Western history.

Fascination with the Queen's value leads novices to avoid early Queen trades (exchanging Queen for Queen). They feel that without the Queen they either can't play at all or the game is less interesting. But the Queen is the most difficult piece of all to handle because it's so gifted. The other side of the coin is that a mistake with the Queen can be terribly costly. So, for one relatively inexperienced, it might be sensible to trade Queens and thereby eliminate some possibilities for serious error. The Queen, in its multifariousness, seems to make the game more stimulating, but so do Rooks, Bishops, and Knights. Anyway, before you can master the Queen, you might better understand the Rook and Bishop, the two pieces that compose the Queen's power. Learn to use all the pieces, not just the Queen.

But can't you violate the principles against weaker opponents?

Base your decisions on the board, not your opponent's strength. Analyze all positions objectively, and then select a course of action. Never play a move you know to be bad or against the spirit of the game. A good idea is good for both a strong player or weak one. A winning game is just that, whatever your rank. Let subjectivity enter your evaluative process and your entire game will suffer—you'll never become a strong player. By playing trappy and risky moves, hoping for an oversight, you're leaving your midsection wide open. Even a beginner has the chance to guess right and refute your play. A good player would never give his opponent such an opportunity.

There are possibly two exceptions:

1) You are an advanced player who has scientifically analyzed your opponent's style and uncovered certain proclivities. The Soviets favor this approach. But even here, it's your objectivity that allows you to exploit his subjectivity. If he seems to mishandle a certain type of position, even if it's not objectively best for you, perhaps there is capital to be made from heading right into it. On an exalted plane, this is what the great Russian Mikhail Botvinnik did at his height.

2) Another time you can play subjectively is when you have a totally lost game. Since eventually you're going to lose anyway, you could take a chance on an inferior but trappy move, hoping your opponent won't understand it or miss your point. In this case, it's really an objective attempt on your part, because you have nothing to lose.

- Never violate a principle without a good reason.
- Play the board, not the opponent.

Occasionally, I (and teachers in the Soviet Union), play an inferior move to see the student's response in the context of a lesson. If he exploits my mistake, I've learned something about his play. If he doesn't, then we can both find out why. Some students complain that this only unearths trivial oversights. It's precisely these small errors that cause them to lose games, however. Before they can reverse these blunders, they must understand why they're making them. Harkening to the methods of Mark Dvoretsky, the great Soviet trainer, I use these pretend situations to develop a student profile, and then I inundate him with corrective exercises and problems based on his failure to spot my purposeful mistakes. In a friendly way, we try to give our students a chance to expose their chessic selves.

If a student capitalizes on my planned blunder, I take the move back and play differently, unless I want to see how he eventually executes his winning plan. This will demonstrate his overall technique. If the student misses my error, I ask him about it and the reasons for his actual move. If his reasons are unclear or unsound, I will talk out the situation with him until everything is understood. If he doesn't know why he played the move he did, then it's obvious he's playing without a plan, a common failing among beginners.

Sometimes an incredibly minor misconception can hold back progress. Once that difficulty is gotten over, the student may be able to make a quantum leap in understanding. The student's ability to ask his own questions, and to find out what's in my mind, can be extremely helpful. The revelations can be startling, especially when the student realizes I never even bothered to consider an idea he thought to be important. He had spent his energy on the irrelevant. For both learning and teaching, turnabout is profitable.

The analysis:
After 1. e4 e5 2. d4 exd4, does White have to take back 3. Qxd4?

No. He instead can sacrifice (see definition in following section) a pawn to gain time for development. Two alternatives are 3. c3 and 3. Nf3. With 3. c3 dxc3 (Black could decline this gambit, for example, and strike back with either 3...Nf6 or 3...d5) 4. Nxc3 (diagram 19), White's compensation for his sacrificed pawn is

DIAGRAM 19

that all his pieces can come out easily with direct threats. Moreover, White's advanced e-pawn and developed Knight are already quite imposing.

White could also play 3. Nf3, threatening to recapture his pawn a move later with his Knight, and he can still offer the gambit (see definition in following section) on move four with 4. c3. Both ideas give White clear attacking possibilities, but they entail somewhat forcing, risky play. Whether White gets enough activity for his gambited pawn is a matter for chess theoreticians to resolve, not beginning players.

After 1. e4 e5 2. d4, should Black take White's pawn or defend his own?

The correct move for Black here is to take White's pawn, for to maintain the initiative, White will have to at least temporarily sacrifice a pawn by 3. c3 or 3. Nf3. If Black were playing passively, he could certainly try 2...Nc6 to defend the e-pawn, but he shouldn't play 2...d6. That would lead to an unfavorable trade of Queens for him and a desirable exchange for White after 3. dxe5 dxe5 4. Qxd8+ Kxd8, when Black has lost the ability to castle and his King remains in the center where it is more vulnerable to White's forces (the center being open). Sometimes this type of exchange is okay, especially when the game verges on the ending and the King will actually be better placed in the center. Mostly it just means that Black must use time making his King safe and therefore will constantly be on the defensive.

• Don't be afraid to trade Queens if it gives you some other kind of advantage.

Sacrifices and Gambitry

A *sacrifice* is the voluntary offer of material for the purpose of gaining a larger advantage, either in material, attack on the enemy King, or some other factor. Often the sacrifice is made in conjunction with a number of moves in a combination. Rudolph Spielmann, in his *Art of Sacrifice in Chess,* said: "The beauty of a game of chess is usually appraised, and with good reason, according to the sacrifices it contains . . . The glowing power of the sacrifice is irresistible: enthusiasm for sacrifice lies in man's nature."

A *gambit* is a voluntary offer, usually of a pawn in the opening, in an attempt to gain another kind of advantage, especially in time. Examples: to gain the attack, increase or seize the initiative, or to improve and add to development.

The most celebrated opening sacrifice of all is the double-edged King's Gambit. Although it can give the gambiteer a powerful initiative, it can also lead to a breach in the protective wall around his own King. Perhaps because he possesses the right blend of daring and poise, some of the greatest victories with the King's Gambit have come at the hands of former world champion Boris Spassky of Russia. The King's Gambit: 1. e4 e5 2. f4.

In *Abinger Harvest*, E. M. Forster professes a fascination for the Evans Gambit, first played in the 1820s by a Welsh sea captain, William Evans. White sacrifices his b-pawn for open lines and central activity. Forster liked this aggressive game, but lacked the knowledge needed to conduct the attack. The Evans Gambit: 1. e4 e5 2. Nf3 Nc6 3. Bc4 Bc5 4. b4.

CHAPTER 3

The Second Moves

White's Second Move

After **1. e4 e5,** I recommend not playing 2. d4, but instead preparing to play this advance at a later time, by first developing the King Knight to the center, **2. Nf3.**

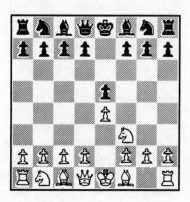

DIAGRAM 20

As this move develops a piece toward the center, it does so with a threat to the Black e-pawn, thus somewhat controlling Black's response. He can't afford to lose a pawn for nothing. He's either got to defend it or play a suitable counterattack.

We've already examined the Petrov Defense (1. e4 e5 2. Nf3 Nf6). It leads to a satisfactory game when handled correctly, but is tough for a beginner to play because of the static nature of the defense. In serious recent games it has been handled by such great players as ex-world champion Tigran Petrosian and former world-class challenger Viktor Korchnoi. But these men obviously have a deeper understanding of the game than the average amateur.

Black's Alternatives

What about defending the e-pawn by 2...f6?

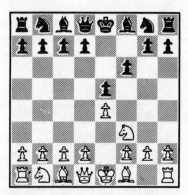

DIAGRAM 21

This is the worst defense Black has. It doesn't contribute to development, deprives the King Knight of its best square (both h6 and e7 offer the Knight fewer options), weakens the h5-e8 diagonal as well as the a2-g8 diagonal (a Bishop posted on this diagonal would prevent Black from castling Kingside, for his King would wind up in check), and generally gives Black a hideous game. Try to avoid unnecessary and weakening pawn moves in the opening, especially if they have nothing else going for them.

The move 2...f6 is actually called Damiano's Defense, named after the Portuguese-Italian master Damiano of the sixteenth century. Although he correctly analyzed 2...f6 as being inferior, somehow the defense was labeled with his name. He was one of the first players to advocate a classical pawn center. Among his maxims for good play are "With an advantage make equal exchanges" (more on this later) and "If you see a good move, look for a better one."

Another try here is 2...Bd6. What do you think of it?

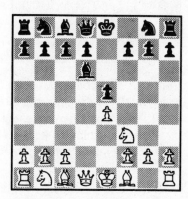

DIAGRAM 22

This move will develop a minor piece toward the center, while protecting the e-pawn, but it leads to its own problem. The Bishop now blocks the Black d-pawn, and one thing you should be able to do in the opening is move both center pawns. After 2...Bd6, Black must find other ways to complete his Queenside development. He will probably lose time and find that his Bishop is awkwardly positioned at d6, literally tied down to the e-pawn's protection, yet eventually vulnerable to pawn and piece play itself. Overall, 2...Bd6 is undesirable.

How about the defense 2...Qf6?

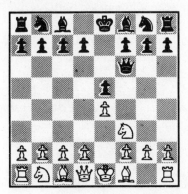

DIAGRAM 23

In addition to usurping Black's best square for his King Knight, it unnecessarily and prematurely develops the Queen in violation of principle. After 3. Nc3, for example, White will be threatening further harassment to her ladyship by 4. Nd5. This (2...Qf6) is overkill. Why have the general do what can be done by the private?

Not much more can be said for 3...Qe7 (diagram 24) either. While it doesn't derail Black's King Knight, it surely impedes Black's King Bishop. It is best to develop your pieces harmoniously, making sure that they don't step on each other's toes. They should be working hand in hand, not against each other. And, of course, don't misuse the Queen. Keep it in readiness for truly desirable circumstances. Since nothing is unusual here, the Queen move is premature.

DIAGRAM 24

What about 2...d6?

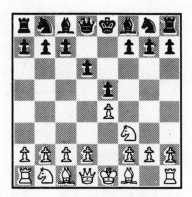

DIAGRAM 25

This is certainly a better move than any of the previous potential defenses. It protects the e-pawn solidly, with a pawn. It also clears the way for the Queen Bishop to enter the fray. If it has any drawback, it's that it slightly obstructs the development of the King Bishop, limiting its immediate scope to the square e7. Thus Black derives a sound but partially cramped game.

The 2...d6 move can produce another problem. It may result in a wasted tempo if Black later should play for d5, which is a key equalizing thrust for Black in so many defenses. Often that advance results in an exchange of Black's d-pawn for White's e-pawn, dissolving the center completely and leading to a more or less equal game. If White has already exchanged his d-pawn for Black's e-pawn, neither side will have a pawn in the center, and both players should have freedom of action for their pieces.

A *leitmotif* (dominant theme) in many e-pawn openings for White is to restrain this freeing advance (Black's d5). As long as White can hold back the Black d-pawn, Black will either be slightly behind in development or have less space or both.

In cases where Black has two center pawns to White's one—as in the Sicilian Defense (1. e4 c5 2. Nf3 d6 3. d4 cxd4 4. Nxd4)—the exchange of Black's d-pawn for White's e-pawn will actually result in Black having the only pawn in the center, thus the best chance of controlling the sector.

The moves 1. e4 e5 2. Nf3 d6 announce Philidor's Defense, named after the great French player François André Danican Philidor (1726–95).

Black's Second Move

 Black continues **2...Nc6.**

DIAGRAM 26

This move does a number of things:

- It protects the e-pawn.
- It doesn't block anything except the Black c-pawn, which doesn't need to be moved here.
- It develops a new piece toward the center.
- It assails the square d4.
- It avoids all of the liabilities raised by the alternative defenses.
- It doesn't weaken anything.

CHAPTER

4

The Third and Fourth Moves

Minor Pieces

So far each side has developed a Knight. Is it advisable to develop Knights early? Generally, yes. This is true for Bishops as well.

It makes sense to bring out the minor pieces (Knights and Bishops) early because they are the easiest to mobilize. After the King- or Queen-pawn has been advanced (or both of them), all the minor pieces already have good squares available on which to settle. The Queen, of course, can become dangerously exposed when developed too early, and it may take awhile to discover the best stations for the Rooks.

Which should you develop first, Knights or Bishops? It's far easier to develop Knights than Bishops because of the former's jumping ability. You can develop both Knights without moving any pawns at all, though this would be extending a sound rule rather too far.

The White King Knight, for example, almost always stands well on the square f3, observing eight different squares simultaneously, which is the best it can do from anywhere. From f3 it may be able to advance later to even more powerful posts in the center. The Bishops have a wider choice of good squares than the Knights, and can therefore delay a bit longer (at least a move or two) before being brought into action.

Since it takes more time for Knights to assume advanced positions, and since it's less committal developing the Knights a little ahead of the Bishops, we have the generally dependable chess axiom:

• Develop Knights before Bishops.

A secondary axiom from our discussion is:

• Develop minor pieces before major pieces.

Principles such as "knights before bishops" are helpful when you can't seem to find your way. You will ask, "What does the principle suggest that I do in this type of situation?" If you can think of a principle that seems to relate, you then take it a step further. You ask, "But does the principle actually apply here?" At this point the principle has served a valuable function as a sounding board for the next move. That's the real value of a principle: to give you a helping hand, to start you thinking. Never use them as absolutes. They are merely guidelines, and subject to exception.

For the purpose of this exposition, it's helpful to divide chess pieces into two classes: the *minor* pieces (Knights and Bishops), and the *major* pieces (Rooks and Queens). These distinctions are based on their exchange values. If we say a pawn is equal to one unit, then:

• A Knight is worth a little more than three pawns.
• A Bishop is worth a fraction more than a Knight (though at the newcomer's level it's impractical to think of Bishops and Knights as being unequal.)
• A Rook is worth about five pawns.
• A Queen is worth about nine pawns.

The chief factor in determining the exchange values is the total number of squares a piece can influence in any given situation.

More About Developing Minor Pieces

Later on, after we introduce the principles on castling, you will find that it's generally good to castle as soon as possible. Castling

Kingside takes less time because the Queen isn't in the way (as it is for Queenside castling). To speed up castling, it's usually better to get out the Kingside minor pieces before the Queenside ones, especially in King-pawn openings where the central region opens up and dilly-dallying around wtih the King in the center can be dangerous.

A common developing scheme for the minor pieces in open games (a game is "open" if movement through the center is not blocked by pawns) is to get them out in the following order:

- The King Knight first
- The King Bishop second
- The Queen Knight third
- The Queen Bishop fourth

This order shouldn't be followed absolutely. In actual games, do what seems best and appropriate. But in a majority of e-pawn openings you'll see that White usually activates his minor pieces in the described fashion.

White's Third Move (the Scotch Game)

The game again: White now plays **3. d4.** He can do so without losing a pawn, for if 3...exd4, White can retake the pawn with his Knight (4. Nxd4). This opening sequence is known as the Scotch Game.

DIAGRAM 27

The Scotch Game (1. e4 e5 2. Nf3 Nc6 3. d4) was first cited in a 1750 book of the Italian master Ercole del Rio. It derived its name from its use and analysis between 1824 and 1829 in several Edinburgh matches and publications. According to Joseph Henry Blackburne (1841-1924), "It gives birth to the sort of position that the young player should study." In contrast, the German grandmaster Dr. Siegbert Tarrasch (1862-1935) referred to it as "bright and lively but at the cost of solidity."

On the surface, the Scotch seems to give White control of the center and quick development. Its drawback is that Black has chances for counterplay against the White e-pawn. Moreover, since Black has not had to play the blocking move d6, he is not as cramped. He also has the opportunity to play the freeing d5 in one move, without having wasted an earlier tempo (if he had moved it one square with d6).

Black's Third Move and White's Response

In our game, Black takes White's d-pawn **3...exd4**(diagram 28) and White takes back with his Knight **4. Nxd4** (diagram 29).

DIAGRAM 28

DIAGRAM 29

Can't Black force White to expose his Queen by 4...Nxd4 5. Qxd4?

DIAGRAM 30

DIAGRAM 31

Yes, Black can bring the White Queen to the center. But unlike the earlier situation (1. e4 e5 2. d4 exd4 3. Qxd4) Black cannot develop with his Queen Knight attacking White's Queen. The Knight has already disappeared in the exchange on move three. Since Black no longer has this resource to attack the White Queen, can he resort to some other time-gainer to exploit the Queen's position?

The only real try to chase the Queen is 5...c5 (diagram 32). That would drive her from the center immediately (possibly to a4—see diagram 33). But 5...c5 doesn't develop a new piece, nor contribute significantly to any other piece's development (it's not so important that the Black Queen now has access to the Queenside along the d8-a5 diagonal). Another problem with this undesirable pawn move is that it severely weakens d5 and d6. These points can never again be guarded by a Black pawn, and White will have an excellent chance to occupy them, especially d5. That one is anchored by a White pawn from e4.

Thus, in taking advantage of the White Queen's central position (diagram 32). Black has to accept a permanent liability—the weak squares along the d-file (diagram 33). A temporary gain in time for an enduring structural weakness is not a fair exchange. At this point, Black's game would be clearly inferior.

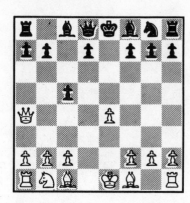

DIAGRAM 32   DIAGRAM 33

Here is an exception to the rule. White can bring out his Queen without disadvantage, all because Black has no effective way to attack it. In the second case, where the Knights have been exchanged (1. e4 e5 2. Nf3 Nc6 3. d4 exd4 4. Nxd4 Nxd4 5. Qxd4), White's Queen can sit in the center, striking out in all directions. But two moves earlier (1. e4 e5 2. d4 exd4 3. Qxd4) it could be dislodged effectively at once.

A slight change can make all the difference, transforming a bad situation into a good one in a single move. A key point, however, is that White didn't have to exert himself to bring out his Queen. Rather, Black helped him by making a bad exchange (4...Nxd4). Taking the pawn is one thing, but trading Knights is another. After exchanging (3...exd4 4. Nxd4) Black should now play a different fourth move.

Black's fourth move could be 4...Bc5, threatening White's Knight.

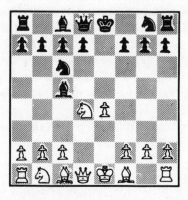

DIAGRAM 34

If so, White's parry could be to play 5. Be3, defending the Knight and preparing a trap for Black. What does White threaten here?

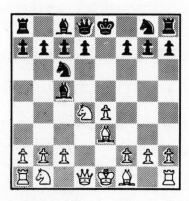

DIAGRAM 35

White threatens 6. Nxc6, capturing Black's Queen Knight while attacking Black's Queen and uncovering an attack to Black's King Bishop. If Black then plays the expected recapture (6...dxc6 or 6. bxc6), White wins a Bishop by 7. Bxc5. With correct play by White at that point, Black would be dead lost.

If White plays badly after winning the Bishop, couldn't Black find a way to come back and win?

He might be able to come back if he plays doggedly and, more particularly, if White plays haphazardly. But that's the point. White would have to discard his advantage. When evaluating a chess position, you should only consider the forces and actions that you can control. In chess, if one side has an extra piece, and the other side has no compensation (as is the case here), the side with greater material will win for sure if played correctly (99 out of 100 cases). All other things being equal, the stronger army wins. It's that simple.

What is the winning technique with an extra piece?

The same as it is in most instances when you're ahead in material: You exchange pieces. This not only emphasizes your advantage (if you trade efficiently, man for man, your extra piece may be the only survivor), you concomitantly reduce the possibility of counterplay. If the opponent has nothing left, he can't attack. So again, exchange pieces—not necessarily pawns—to win when ahead in material.

Instead of 4...Bc5, What's wrong with 4...Bb4 + ?

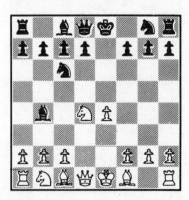

DIAGRAM 36

Plenty. It develops a piece, but not usefully. It gives a check, but not menacingly. White can get out of check pronto with 5.c3, and the bishop must move again, wasting time. A move that gives check isn't necessarily a good one. A bad check can lose time, and on some occasions, even a game.

Because checking moves appear so forceful, however, they're irresistible to many players. Automatic checks are meaningless. They sometimes lose games. Suppose, for example, one of your men is attacked, and instead of countering that threat, you choose instead to check the enemy King. If your opponent responds to your check with a move that contains another threat (such as a King move that attacks a second one of your pieces or pawns) you will then need to cope with two threats: the new one, and the one you didn't answer to begin with. Chances are you'll solve only one of your problems, not both.

Don't give check simply because you can. Check because it's necessary or useful in accomplishing one of your objectives, just as any other move.

• Don't give pointless checks.

Black's Fourth Move

After **1. e4 e5 2. Nf3 Nc6 3. d4 exd4 4. Nxd4:**

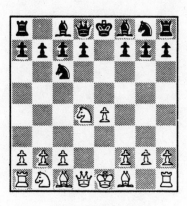

As in our earlier description of the Scotch game, White appears to have his way in the center, with both a Knight (d4) and a pawn (e4) occupying central squares. Black has nothing yet in the center, but he's attacking the White Knight at d4, which is presently defended. And with his next move, Black can try to take some of the initiative with an attack against White's e-pawn.

Black plays **4...Nf6.**

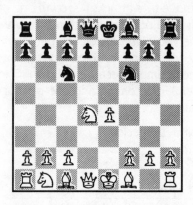

DIAGRAM 37

Black has now developed a piece toward the center with a gain of time in that he's threatening to take White's e-pawn.

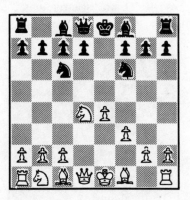

The Fifth Moves

White's Alternatives

White considers four possible responses. Defending the pawn by either f3, Qd3, or Nc3, or first exchanging Knights on c6 and then defending the pawn. Let's examine each of the answers.

What about 5. f3?

DIAGRAM 38

This move echoes many of the attendant problems of Black's 2...f6. It loses time in not developing a new piece, nor does it clear a line allowing new pieces to come into play (as does moving the e- and d-pawns).

And it weakens the h4-e1 diagonal leading to the King. If White should now castle, his King becomes potentially vulnerable along the g1-a7 diagonal (say by a Black Bishop from c5). It's just not an effective way to cope with the threat. White wants to secure his e-pawn while continuing to build his game—this doesn't do it.

The following game, played in a Soviet classroom between eleven-year-olds during my visit in 1984, offers an illustration of what happens when this choice is made:

1. e4 e5 2. Nf3 Nc6 3. d4 exd4 4. Nxd4 Nf6 5. f3 Bc5 (immediately trying to seize the weakened diagonal) 6. Nb3? (unnecessarily opening the diagonal; better would have been 6. Be3, threatening to win a piece by first capturing on c6 and then taking the Bishop at c5) 6...Bb6 7. Bb5? (a pointless attack on the Knight) 7...0-0 (here, Black could have already sacrificed on e4, opening up White's debilitated position) 8. Bxc6? (another pointless move, adding to White's woes by giving Black's light-square Bishop a chance to assume the powerful a6-f1 diagonal) 8...bxc6 9. a4? (hoping to trap the Bishop by a subsequent a5, but at the cost of development and the game itself) 9...Nxe4 10. fxe4 Qh4+ 11. g3 Qxe4+ 12. Kd2 (better was the also losing 11. Qe2) 12...Qe3 mate.

DIAGRAM 39

As for 5. Qd3...

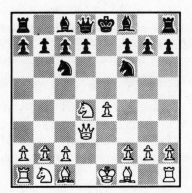

DIAGRAM 40

This problem is a little different. Though not a bad move, it unnecessarily relies on the Queen. At d3 the Queen blocks in White's light-square Bishop, while being overburdened with the defense of the d4 and e4 squares. Try not to use the Queen so much in the opening. If possible, develop your lighter pieces first, then you're ready for the Queen's participation.

What about interposing 5. Nxc6 first?

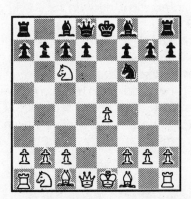

DIAGRAM 41

This is actually a strong continuation. White can play 5. Nxc6 first, before defending his e-pawn, because it more or less forces Black's response, which is to take back the Knight. Otherwise,

Black loses a piece, and faces an additional attack on his Queen. After 5...bxc6, for example, White can then secure his e-pawn. By making the first exchange he lost no time and actually made it easier to defend his center, for now the Knight that used to be at d4 no longer has to be guarded. This raises a new principle:

• Sometimes you can gain time by exchanging pieces.

You could rid yourself of the necessity of having to do something, like provide protection. If an attacked piece is exchanged away, you needn't worry about it anymore, and if you've gotten truly equal value for it, you've lost nothing. After the exchange, you can go on with your game.

A limitation on this is if, in exchanging, you build your opponent's game. Then you've gained no time at all, but actually lost it. Examples: if you trade a developed piece for an undeveloped one, or if you trade and develop an enemy piece in the process. Don't trade without a purpose. A good trade can gain time. A bad one can lose it.

A popular continuation from 5. Nxc6 was developed by Nikolai Kopayev (1914-78, Soviet master and railway technician): 5...bxc6 6. e5 (if 6. Bd3, then 6...d5 7. Nd2! Bc5 8. 0-0 0-0 9. Qf3 Ng4 10. exd5 Qd6; or 6...d5 7. e5 Ng4 8. 0-0 Bc5 9. Bf4 f6 10. exf6 0-0!, with an excellent position for Black) 6...Qe7 7. Qe2 Nd5 8. c4 Ba6 9. Nd2!.

The move 5. Nxc6, played before coping with the threat to White's e-pawn with the idea of saving White's e-pawn a move later, is known as a *zwischenzug* (a German term that means "in-between move"). It was played in between a set of other moves, without necessarily effecting the first sequence. It refers to moves that are played by choice instead of being apparently forced responses. They often come as a surprise, though 5. Nxc6 is hardly that.

White's Fifth Move; Black's Response

So White could play 5. Nxc6 quite satisfactorily, but he doesn't. Instead he protects his e-pawn by **5. Nc3**, which also develops a new piece toward the center.

DIAGRAM 42

 Here Black continues his development with **5...Bb4**. In addition to preparing to castle, what does this move threaten?

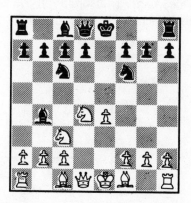

DIAGRAM 43

It attacks the Knight on c3, though many players might feel that nothing is really threatened, for the Knight is adequately protected by the b-pawn. But that's only part of the story. The Bishop actually pins the Knight to White's King. The Knight can't move without exposing its own King to attack, which is illegal.

What Is a Pin?

A pin is one of the five main tactics in chess (the other four being forks, skewers, discoveries, and underminings). It's a tactic by which one piece attacks two enemy pieces along the same line (rank, file, or diagonal), so that if the front enemy man moves, it will expose the second enemy man to capture. In all pins, the first enemy man (the one that's pinned) is less important than the second enemy man (the piece it is pinned to).

Here it is said the Rook pins the Bishop to the King. Or the Bishop is pinned to the King by the Rook. The key to this tactic is that the front enemy man is helpless. It simply cannot move away. This is known as an *absolute pin*. A *relative pin* is shown in diagram 45. Black can move his pinned Rook away if he's willing to sacrifice his Queen. But in diagram 44, the absolute pin, he couldn't move his pinned piece away even if he wanted to.

DIAGRAM 44

DIAGRAM 45

Since pieces stuck in absolute pins are truly helpless to move away even if threatened further, it might make sense not to capture them right away. Rather you may want to intensify the pressure by attacking them with additional force, especially a pawn. Thus, this principle:

• You should try to attack pinned pieces and pawns again and again (if you have the time and correct circumstances) until they can be won.

In diagram 46, we see a situation where piling up on a pinned piece can occur. Instead of capturing Black's Rook at c6 with his Bishop at a4, winning only the exchange (a Rook for a Bishop), White should push his d-pawn, attacking the helpless Rook. White will thereby have to surrender merely a pawn to capture the Rook, not a Bishop. It's this threat to attack pinned pieces with lesser material that gives the tactic much of its strength.

DIAGRAM 46

CHAPTER 6

The Sixth Moves

Back to the game. The Knight at c3 is pinned absolutely to White's King. The result: the Knight is no longer guarding the pawn on e4, which means Black is once again threatening to capture it.

Several things should be noted here. One is that a dark-square Bishop (the one on b4), by pinning the Knight, is actually attacking the pawn on e4. Remember: Bishops can assail squares of the other color by attacking pieces that guard those squares (in particular, Knights). Another point is the way this affects the center. Having already seen that one can occupy or guard the center, we now encounter a third way to approach it: to attack or drive away enemy men that guard it. Influencing the center in this way can be just as vital as occupying or controlling it.

How should White save his e-pawn? We've already reviewed the moves f3 and Qd3, and even though a move has passed, they're really just as wanting as before. Another possibility is 6. Bd3. This is a fine developing move, but here it has a severe drawback. It blocks the Queen's defense to d4.

Is there some way White can cope with this threat to his Knight and still be able to develop his bishop to d3, guarding the e-pawn?

If White tries to move his Knight away, say to b5 or b3, that would waste a move and Black would merely capture the e-pawn (Nxe4). The same would result if White were to expend a tempo by defending the Knight at d4 with 6. Be3. Again Black would just take the pawn. The only Knight move for White that gains time is to capture Black's Knight, **6. Nxc6.** After Black plays the natural and virtually forced recapture on c6, White can go ahead and defend his e-pawn. This exchange falls into the category of in-between move or zwischenzug.

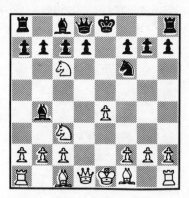

DIAGRAM 47

• Remember the principle: Exchange to gain time.

Now the question is, how should Black recapture the Knight? By 6...bxc6 or by 6...dxc6? Let's consider first 6...dxc6.

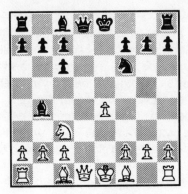

DIAGRAM 48

One advantage to taking back this way is that Black keeps his pawns together in two groups (group 1: h7, g7, f7; group 2: c6, c7, b7, a7). After 6...bxc6, his pawns then reside in three groups: h7, g7, f7; d7, c6, c7; and a7.

Generally, it's better if your pawns exist in as few groups (or *pawn islands,* as they're called) as possible.

However, a disadvantage of 6...dxc6 is that it allows White to trade Queens, unfavorable for Black. After 7. Qxd8 + Kxd8, Black has lost the right to castle. His King then remains exposed and vulnerable.

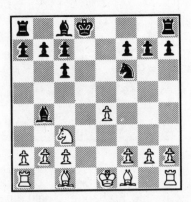

DIAGRAM 49

Generally, capture so that you are opening lines for your pieces to come out, as with 6...dxc6 in the game possibility, which would permit the development of the Queen Bishop through the center. Yes, 6...bxc6 also opens a line for the Queen Bishop, the c8-a6 diagonal. But usually mobility increases when you can develop through the center. Consider especially the opening of the central files in conjunction with letting out the Queen Bishop resulting from 6...dxc6. Again, 6...bxc6 also gives an open file, the b-file which can be used by Black's Queen Rook.

Nevertheless, when you capture to improve mobility you may be increasing the number of pawn islands or groups. Again it comes down to a matter of balancing what you get for what you give up. Surprisingly, Black's best move here is 6...bxc6.

Let's Digress: Steinitz's Views

That a chess game hinges on a delicate equilibrium of forces and elements was first propounded by the Viennese master Wilhelm Steinitz (1836-1900). To achieve an advantage in one of these elements you had to surrender another kind of advantage of about equal worth (or: you don't get something for nothing in a well-balanced chess game).

Winning a pawn could easily cost you several moves in development. You might have to move your attacking piece into position, capture the enemy man, and then move your own man back to safety. It's cost you three moves to win a pawn. For a material advantage you had to cede a possibly equalizing advantage in time. Your opponent might then be able in those three moves to build up an attack with his probable initiative. Was it worth it?

Steinitz realized that the overall advantage is dependent on a number of factors, though at any given moment, one type of factor may be more important than another. These factors, which tend to be in a state of flux, are essentially of two kinds: tangible and intangible. Advantages in material or *pawn structure* (the way the pawns are dispersed over the board, taking into account their weaknesses and strengths, and the way they create harmony or disharmony for the pieces) are tangible. Unless a major upheaval takes place, these factors are likely to remain unchanged throughout the course of a game. A lead in development, however, is transitory. If you don't exploit it immediately, your advantage will evaporate once your opponent completes his development by getting out the rest of his pieces.

A key factor in the opening, as already indicated, is time, or more specifically, the *initiative*. White tries to convert his first-move advantage into something concrete by maintaining the initiative, and Black attempts to equalize by taking the initiative away. In the fight for the initiative, contemporary players, especially those of the Soviet school, will try almost anything—if it works. Not only will they make serious concessions by accepting weaknesses and ceding space, but often they commit themselves to risky material sacrifices, such as opening gambits of pawns and even pieces.

Okay, so how is a chess game won?

This may seem absurd on the surface, but if both players are on top of things, probably neither one will be able to win merely by making direct forcing moves. For everything that one side can do, the other side has a counterbalancing action to keep the game in equilibrium. Theoretically, the game should be drawn (someday a computer may show us otherwise).

Still, one sits down to win at chess, not to draw. To win, you must follow a course of action that increases your winning chances. Steinitz put forth the idea of playing for small advantages—so apparently insignificant that either your opponent doesn't see you're getting them, or he does and judges they're not important enough to worry him. None of these atom-sized advantages will mean very much at the time, but if you accumulate enough of them they may add up to a gargantuan superiority.

Suddenly you've got a powerful initiative. Your opponent, to break this initiative, must in turn surrender something, usually material. You capture the material and the game may again come back to an equilibrium where neither player has an immediate attacking advantage. But there's one telling difference: You now have extra material—in a sense you have literally stolen it from your opponent because you never had to make legitimate sacrifices for it.

• Playing for small advantages is what strong players do. It's called *positional chess.*

The famous Soviet teacher Alexander Kotov (1913-81) listed seventeen factors of the small nature. Echoing chemistry, he arranged them in what he called a "Mendeleev table." The factors include things like controlling a file; having the better minor piece (in blocked positions, probably a Knight; in open positions, probably a Bishop); having slightly better piece placement, slightly stronger pawns, slightly more space; and so on. Acquire a number of these slight edges and you have an enormous advantage.

The Russian chemist Dmitri Mendeleev (1835-1907), was actually a quite fine chessplayer who once defeated the great Mikhail Chigorin in a game. An example of his skill is the following position. With the White pieces he was able to win the Black Queen. Do you see how?

DIAGRAM 50

Mendeleev played 1. Bh7+, discovering an attack on the Black Queen. After 1...Kxh7, he won with 2. Qxd6.

What is a discovered attack?

Discovered attacks (see chapter 7), or just plain discoveries, are tactical devices that occur when you move one of your men off a particular line (rank, file, or diagonal) so that another man suddenly is able to capture an enemy man. Although the stationary unit gives the discovered attack, the moving unit may deliver a serious threat too. When the stationary man uncorks a discovered attack to the enemy King, its called *discovered check*. In those cases the moving attacker has a virtual carte blanche to attack or capture anything because the discovered check must be responded to. When both the moving and stationary attackers give check it's called *double check*. These tactics can result in sudden catastrophe, as in diagram 51.

DIAGRAM 51

In diagram 51, White mates in one move by 1.Bb5 double check and mate. Black cannot block both checks with one move. (The White King doesn't appear in the diagram because it's not relevant to the pattern.)

Structural Weakness

One main thing positional chess is concerned with is *weakness*. In chess there are really two kinds of weaknesses. One type involves points or sectors of the board that are tactically vulnerable only because of immediate circumstances. They shouldn't be evaluated as part of a long-term plan. Usually you have to capitalize on a tactical weakness at once to prevent your opponent from rectifying the problem by guarding the weak point, removing a threatened piece, or whatever.

The other type of weakness is structural and what Steinitz had in mind for his positional chess theory and what most people think of as weaknesses. They involve badly placed pawns. The pawns can no longer guard certain squares either because they have advanced too far or because they are unable to exercise their protective ability (they could be pinned, for example). Because structural weaknesses tend to be of a lasting nature, they must be considered when formulating long-range plans.

Basic to the problem is the isolated pawn, often a disadvantage because it can't be protected by other pawns and also because the square in front can be occupied by opposing pieces. Without a friendly pawn to the side to guard the occupied square, there's no guarantee of driving the blockading piece away. Pieces able to sit in front of isolated pawns are called *blockaders,* and the concept is usually referred to as the *blockade.*

DIAGRAM 52

Diagram 52 shows four isolated pawns: two for White, two for Black. White has isolated pawns at d4 and f5, Black at b6 and b7. Black's isolated pawns are doubled on the b-file and are called *doubled isolated pawns.* White's doubled pawns on the b-file are not isolated because they have an adjacent partner on the a-file, which, under the right circumstances, can defend either White b-pawn. Healthy pawns are represented by Black's three on the squares e7, f7, and g7. They are *connected pawns,* being on adjacent files.

DIAGRAM 53

Diagram 53 shows how a blockading piece (the Knight) can sit securely on the square in front of an isolated pawn (White's pawn on f4). To dislodge the Knight on f5 White needs a pawn on either the e- or g-file.

There are times, however, when an isolated pawn (or "isolani") can offer compensation. In fact, some openings are designed to produce an isolated pawn center. A player might accept such a pawn—normally a handicap—if in the process he gets more space, control of useful strong points, or the opportunity to exert a hampering effect over the enemy's position.

Perhaps the best example of a weakness that can be accompanied by offsetting advantages is the double-pawn complex. Despite its obvious drawbacks, the appearance of doubled pawns generally signals the creation of open lines, and especially if it comes about because a Bishop is surrendered for a Knight, creating greater attacking chances. This doesn't mean that doubled pawns are not inherently weak—they are. But like everything else in chess, they must be judged in relation to other factors. At times, it's even possible that doubled pawns can be superior to so-called healthy ones.

There are other types of pawn weaknesses too—backward pawns, doubled-isolated pawns, tripled pawns, hanging pawns, the isolated pawn pair, and so on. In all such cases, the pawns are weak because they are unable to guard certain squares, either in actuality or for practical reasons preventing them from doing so.

Black's Sixth Move

Black plays **6...bxc6.** This avoids the exchange of Queens, and it also isolates the a-pawn, which might become a severe weakness in the endgame. But this is not an endgame yet, thus certain factors such as isolated rook pawns here are not yet as important. To repeat, all factors vary in value depending on the circumstances. The capture points out a new rule: If you can make either of two pawn captures, away from or toward the center, capture toward the center as Black does here. It's chiefly advantageous in that it puts several Black pawns in the center, giving Black an excellent chance to control the central region. Generally, the more pawns you have in the center, the better your chances of controlling it. Taking back this way also avoids giving White an unfavorable advantage in pawn balances.

DIAGRAM 54

Pawn Majorities

If, over a given number of files, you have more pawns than your opponent you have what is called a *pawn majority*. The chief advantages of pawn majorities is that they give you better chances of controlling a region and provide you with the opportunity to create a *passed pawn* (a pawn that cannot be stopped by any enemy pawn from moving up the board to Queen—it's literally passed the opposition's pawns). By playing 6...dxc6 (diagram 55), Black would be giving his opponent the equivalent of an extra pawn.

It works like this:

DIAGRAM 55

DIAGRAM 56

On the Kingside, White has four pawns to Black's three. With proper play White will be able to squeeze through a passed pawn on the King file. (In advancing these pawns, by the way, follow Capablanca's rule: start by advancing the unopposed pawn, the pawn with no enemy pawn in front of it. This pawn is likely to become a new queen and is called the *candidate*.)

White here is up a pawn so far in our analysis. On the Queenside Black has the extra pawn, but he also has doubled pawns on the c-file. His four pawns can be held back by White's three pawns (see diagram below). In effect, White is up a pawn. If you exchange the wrong way, creating favorable imbalances for your opponent, you may find yourself tantamount to a pawn down. The move 6...bxc6, (diagram 56) prevents the possibility of the e-pawn squeezing through along the e-file. There is now no way for White to create a passed pawn by force.

Another advantage to taking toward the center here **(6...bxc6)**, is that Black then gets an open b-file for his Rook. At the right moment he can shift his Rook to b8, either threatening to capture the b-pawn (if it's no longer defended), or forcing White to make a special effort to get his Bishop out (if he moves it, he leaves the b-pawn hanging when the Rook is at b8). The usual way to defend such a pawn is to push it one square, so that its neighboring pawns then guard it.

But here's a problem. With the pawn on b3 instead of b2, the squares a3 and c3 are weakened. No longer protected by a pawn, they are susceptible to Black's forces. Moreover, after the advance b3, Black may be able to exert annoying pressure along the h8-a1 diagonal, either from his dark-square bishop or his queen by transferring either of them to that diagonal. Additionally, in some positions, with the Rook at b8, it may be able to enter the fray by shifting up to b4, attacking White's e-pawn.

Seize Open Lines

Bishops, Rooks, and Queens are long-range pieces. They can strike suddenly from a distance, but need avenues of attack. They seek open lines: ranks, files, and diagonals unobstructed by pawns of the same color. (You are said to *control* a line when you occupy it with a piece that can move along it freely.)

It's important to secure control of open lines before your opponent does. Capture these vital highways and then reinforce your conquest by occupying them with two or more pieces that move in the same way. If trying to dominate a diagonal, use a Bishop and a Queen. If attempting to commandeer ranks and files, use either a Rook and Queen or two Rooks. You're thereby in control of these critical rows because the pieces that occupy their squares protect and support one another. The doubling of like forces in this manner along the same row of squares is called a *battery*. Try, wherever possible, to set up batteries and other forms of double attack.

The effectiveness of this strategy is illustrated by doubled Rooks—two Rooks stationed on the same file or rank. One very devastating battery in chess is a pair of Rooks doubled on the seventh rank. With this, the enemy often has a vulnerable row of pawns ripe for capture. Beat your opponent to the punch: seize important open lines as soon as you can, and then control them as long as possible.

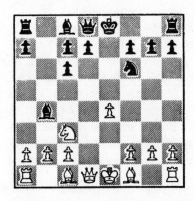

The Seventh Moves

King Safety

Again White must defend his e-pawn.

Although the Knight at c3 is in position to guard it, the Bishop at b4 pins the Knight to its King. It can't move and the pawn at e4 is really hanging (attacked and unprotected). Can White save his pawn by breaking the pin with 7. Bd2? Doesn't that free the Knight to again protect the pawn?

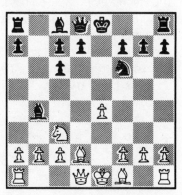

DIAGRAM 57

The move 7. Bd2 certainly resolves the pin, and now the Knight can move if given a chance. There's a problem, though. Black's 5...Bb4 wasn't just a pin. It also was a threat to capture the Knight, reducing control of e4. So after castling, to get the King to safety, Black threatens to play Bxc3 followed by Nxe4. Now White must still find another defense for his e-pawn. Moreover, Bd2 is really too passive a deployment of the Queen Bishop. All it does from d2 is break a pin, whereas it could assume a mightier post at g5, where it would do the pinning instead of providing a buffer against one. So Bd2 is not a really strong idea here.

 White instead played the natural developing move, **7. Bd3.**

DIAGRAM 58

This is sound development, and prepares for Kingside castling, while positioning the Bishop along a good diagonal (d3-h7). The move also temporarily solidifies White's e-pawn.

Black now has a number of reasonable moves. He could strike back in the center by 7...d5 or he could castle 7...0-0. He might also consider 7...d6, to restrain White's e-pawn, but this is comparatively passive. A curious try, which to many might seem like a good idea, is 7...Bxc3 + .

DIAGRAM 59

This might seem attractive because after 8. bxc3, White is left with doubled isolated pawns. They would be particularly weak in the endgame, along with the isolated White e-pawn. But Black may not get the chance to reach the endgame to exploit White's pawn weaknesses.

Surely, wherever feasible give your opponent pawn weaknesses, such as doubled and isolated pawns. But don't do it if in the process you will incur terrible disadvantages. Limit the emphasis on doubled pawns. There's a lot more to chess than just that, such as the increased activity and open attacking lines your opponent gets from some of these exchanges.

Black's Bishop will probably be more important to him than White's Knight to White. If Black meant to take the Knight on c3 with his Bishop, it would be more sensible to do it after White's dark-square Bishop had first been developed, say to g5. But since the Bishop at c1 hasn't yet moved, it can shift to a3 in one play— made possible by the unwise exchange of Bishop for Knight, clearing the c1-a3 diagonal.

From a3, the Bishop could wreak havoc, cutting across the board into the heart of the Black camp. Note, with the Bishop at a3, Black is unable to castle, unless he can manage to block the Bishop's diagonal (say, by d6). If he's already moved his d-pawn two squares, to d5 (diagram 60), it would be impossible to cut the Bishop's line. At that point, Black's game would be hopeless. As we shall soon see, it's generally desirable to prevent your opponent from castling.

DIAGRAM 60

Castling

A sure sign of chess naïveté is the repeated failure to castle from game to game. Actually, it's usually desirable to castle as soon as possible, for two reasons:

- It gets the King to safety.
- It develops a Rook.

Quick losses often result when a King is caught in the center with little or no protection, exposed to a withering attack along the lines that have been opened by the advance of the center pawns. Castling safeguards the King by sheltering it behind a wall of pawns, especially if you haven't violated the spirit of sound opening play and made too many pawn moves. The need for a safe haven for the King explains castling's defensive side.

Castling can be an attacking move too. It's usually the most convenient way to bring out the Rooks. Rooks should be posted on:

- Open files, containing no pawns whatsoever.
- Half-open files, containing only enemy pawns.
- Files containing advanced pawns that may soon be exchanged.
- Files containing pawns you intend to advance.

A Rook cannot penetrate into enemy territory if the file on which it stands is obstructed by one of its own pawns. Enemy pawns in its own path are another matter—they can easily become targets for attack. A Rook is not really hindered if its own pieces (not pawns) block the way, for they usually can be moved off the file. Pawns can't automatically do this because they only move on files. To clear them away, you have to exchange them for enemy pieces and/or pawns.

Castling:

- Brings one Rook closer to the center.
- Also vacates a useful square for the other Rook.

Often asked is the question: Is it better to castle Kingside or Queenside? It depends. Most times you will castle Kingside because it can happen sooner (there's one less piece to get out of the way—the Queen), not because it's better. The real dilemma doesn't arise until you actually have the chance to castle either way. You might decide which by asking certain questions. For example, will the King be safer on the Kingside or on the Queenside? Well, which side has the best cover of protective pawns? (It's usually safer to castle where the pawns have not been moved.) And which side has the greatest concentration of opposing forces? (You'll usually want to castle on the other side, away from the bigger army.) There may be more subtle reasons as well, but these tend to be less crucial than the two already given. These factors are paramount in making a choice.

Since early castling is so desirable, we can appreciate another reason to develop minor pieces so quickly. The squares separating the King from one of the Rooks must be unoccupied before castling is possible. The minor pieces must be developed just to create the potential for castling. For example, if your King is going to be threatened on the next move, it can be very helpful to have the option of castling. If two pieces still block the way, however, it's impossible to protect yourself by castling immediately and your King may wind up stuck in the center (good luck . . . you'll need it).

A useful corollary therefore is that it can be effective strategy to prevent your opponent from castling. To this end:

• Try to keep the enemy King pinned down in the center.
• Try to hit the enemy King with a combined assault of all your pieces.
• Be willing to sacrifice some material in order to do this, if your chances seem menacing.
• Once done, don't relent. Keep hammering away to prevent your opponent from regrouping and organizing a defense.

In our game: Black castles **7...0-0.**

DIAGRAM 61

White must be careful. If he keeps his King centralized, Black may have time to actively harass along the e-file by shifting his Rook to e8. When the e-file is at least half-open to the enemy's advantage, it's potentially dangerous to leave your King sitting on its original square. Here, though White's e-pawn would screen the White King from Black's pressuring rook at e8, the threats against the then pinned pawn might become quite serious. Then White might become overtaxed, trying to extricate his King to safe quarters while also securing his menaced e-pawn. There's an old Yiddish expression that goes, "You can't dance at two weddings at the same time." It's application here is that you may not be able to cope with contemporaneous threats. Look for double threats, both on attack and defense. Try to avoid situations where you will be faced with dual responsibilities.

To illustrate our point about the precarious state of White's position along the e-file, consider the case where White continues with 8. a3? (diagram 62), unnecessarily menacing the Bishop and in fact wasting time. (Don't make unnecessary pawn moves.)

After 8. a3, Black willingly exchanges Bishop for Knight (8...Bxc3 9. bxc3), which gains vital time because it is now Black's move to go ahead with his plans. If he had retreated his Bishop instead, say to a5, it would then be White's move and Black

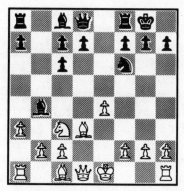

DIAGRAM 62

would not have benefited. Remember, exchanging pieces can often gain time.

Black could now commence operations against the e-pawn. The slow way, but here not ineffective, would be to seize the e-file with 9...Re8. Black would be threatening the e-pawn twice, and White, then only defending the pawn once, would have to expend a tempo to protect it again.

But Black has a much more expeditious attacking weapon, the immediate capture of the e-pawn with his Knight, 9...Nxe4!.

DIAGRAM 63

After the obvious 10. Bxe4, Black can regain the piece by 10...Re8, pinning the Bishop to the King. Even if White should defend his Bishop with a pawn by 11. f3, Black merely attacks the helplessly pinned unit with his own pawn (say 11...f5 (or 11...d5 too), and next move recaptures it. If White moves out of the pin by the natural 12.0-0, Black winds up a pawn ahead after 12...fxe4 13. fxe4 Rxe4.

This variation reinforces several ideas. It shows the problem with unnecessary pawn moves (they waste time); it shows the difficulties ensuing from a delay of castling after the other side has castled and therefore is prepared for full scale attacking operations (the King may be stuck in the center); it also illustrates the value of pins (there's no immediate need to capture the pinned piece—in many cases you have time to attack the pinned unit again, hopefully with a pawn).

Look for Double Attacks

Double attacks are very common in chess. They're the most usual way in which material is won. The simplest kind of double attack is a *fork*. It occurs when one friendly man attacks two or more opposing men on the same move. Diagram 64 illustrates a Knight fork. White wins the Queen by 1. Ng6 +, forking the King and Queen. After the King moves away, the Knight takes the Queen.

DIAGRAM 64

Other types of double attacks that happen frequently are pins and discovered attacks (explained earlier), skewers, and undermining. A *skewer* is the opposite of a pin. In a pin, one man threatens two enemy men along its line of power, where the less valuable of the two enemy men shields the more valuable from attack (See diagram 65). In a skewer, the more valuable is generally in front of the less valuable and must get out of the way, exposing the enemy man behind to capture (See diagram 66).

DIAGRAM 65

DIAGRAM 66

Undermining involves removing the protection for an enemy man by capturing its support or driving it away. This tactic is also referred to as *removing the defender* or *removing the guard*. In diagram 67, White wins either a Bishop or a Knight by 1. Bxc6,

DIAGRAM 67

removing the protection for the Bishop at e5. If Black plays 1...bxc6, White wins the Bishop with 2. Nxe5. And if Black tries to save his Bishop by moving it away, then White saves his Bishop at c6, moving it away. Here, though, Black lost the Knight on c6.

Discovered attacks were shown earlier (see chapter 6). They hinge on a friendly man moving out of the way of another friendly man so that an enemy man could be exposed to capture. In diagram 68, Black wins the White Queen by either 1...Nd2 + or 1...Nc3 +, in both cases discovering an attack from the Bishop to the King.

DIAGRAM 68

Having to defend against two or more simultaneous threats can pose a real predicament, especially if one of the threatened men is the King. Most double attacks, however, don't happen of themselves. They are more often the logical outcome of a carefully planned assault. The idea is to maneuver purposefully until you see a way to combine two threats against the enemy position into a single powerful move. Get into the habit of planning ahead. Always keep an eye open for double attacks, and watch your play improve.

II

Middle Game

The Eighth and Ninth Moves

 White castles **8. 0-0.**

DIAGRAM 69

Black could continue here with 8...d6, opening the way for his Queen Bishop and guarding e5, which restrains White's e-pawn. Though that would stop an immediate movement of the White e-pawn, White would still have a spatial advantage in the center because his center pawn is then further advanced than Black's at d6. With more room for his pieces, and more options, White could find himself with a comfortable initiative.

But Black chooses a different strategy. He plays **8...d5,** with the idea of liquidating White's e-pawn and getting a fair share of the center.

DIAGRAM 70

On the surface, Black is attacking the White e-pawn twice, once with his Knight and once with his pawn. The pawn, however, appears to be defended twice, by the Knight and Bishop. Generally, when like defenders are involved, a point is adequately protected when the number of defenders equals the number of attackers. This is not necessarily true when unlike attackers and defenders are facing each other. For example, if two enemy pawns are threatening a friendly pawn defended in toto by a Queen, Rook, Bishop, and Knight, the friendly pawn is not adequately guarded. If either enemy pawn captures it, none of the friendly pieces can take it back without the sacrifice of material. Whichever one takes back will be captured in turn by an enemy pawn, which in value is far inferior to a Knight or any other piece.

Counting Material

One of the most basic calculations you have to make in a chess game concerns material. Not only will you, from time to time, decide who's ahead (though you should always keep a general idea of that in your head), but on any given exchange, you'll want to know how you're going to fare. Whether you exchange or not depends on the value of the material.

This is fairly easy to calculate. Material can be tangibly seen, counted, and compared. An intangible element like time is more difficult to evaluate. The initiative (a lead in time that allows you to direct the flow of play) is not really measurable. But chessmen can actually be given reasonably concrete values based on the number of squares they influence and how they do it. For convenience, such values are expressed in terms of the weakest unit, the pawn.

By approximation, Knights and Bishops are worth roughly a fraction more than three pawns each, with Bishops generally a twinge more valuable than Knights. Rooks are worth about five pawns each, and the Queen about nine. You may appreciate these comparisons better if you avoid using the word "points." Don't say a Knight is worth three points. Say it's worth three pawns. This means, in an exchange of a Knight for pawns to come out even, the Knight should get three pawns in the transaction.

Values Are Not Constant

These values are somewhat relative, however, being subject to the changing fortunes of the game. The worth of a piece may fluctuate slightly from position to position, and in extreme cases, the change can be quite great. A pawn that reaches the back rank to become a new Queen by force is surely more valuable than a feckless Knight, removed from the main theater. But for determining the worthiness of most captures and exchanges, the usual values can be trusted.

As a rule, unless exchanging brings you nonmaterial compensation (for example, an attack against the enemy King) you will want to get back at least as much material as you give up.

When evaluating an exchange of material, after you count and total the pieces and pawns, then compare them. Usually I begin with the pawns for each side. I do the same for each type of piece (grouping Bishops and Knights together under the broader category of minor pieces), and noting the differences, rather than adding everything up. If, at the end of the calculation, I see that Black has an extra Bishop but White has an extra two pawns, I note that Black is slightly ahead. I will not say that Black is about a pawn ahead (three for two), but rather that he has a Bishop for two pawns, or that White has two pawns for a Bishop. I may even say that Black has a piece for two pawns (where piece always means minor piece, not ever a Rook or a Queen).

In these calculations, I would never say that Black is ahead a pawn, because that doesn't really convey an accurate picture of the position. Being ahead a pawn in this sense could mean:

- One side has an extra pawn.
- One side could have a Bishop, the other two pawns.
- One side could have a Rook, the other a Knight and a pawn.
- One side could have a Queen, the other a Rook and Bishop.
- One side could have two Rooks, the other a Queen.

Each of these situations is different, and each requires a different plan of action for both sides. To say that one is down one pawn to describe all of these situations is both confusing and meaningless.

If you want to avoid muddled reasoning in your own games, always express material differences in concrete, specific terms. State exactly how much material you have (or are getting), and what your opponent has for it (or is getting).

A habit to avoid: Don't calculate by counting the chessmen next to the board on the side. Yes, these are usually the men already captured in the game, but they may not be all of them. Pieces could become misplaced or lost, fouling up your calculation. Wily or waggish opponents might even hide a few chessmen, especially if they know you're prone to this bad habit. And if you're playing in a club or tournament, neighboring sets tend to mix with your own, complicating rather than simplifying your task.

It's also bad form to count this way. Do you look to the side to find a brilliant combination, or to find your next move? When you're playing chess, the board is your universe. All your information should come from there and nowhere else.

- Always play the board—not the person, not the side.

The game again: After 8...d5, is Black threatening to win material?

Yes, not by capturing White's e-pawn right away, but by first reducing the number of defenders of the pawn via the exchange of Bishop on b4 for Knight on c3. If given the opportunity (say White plays an irrelevant move), Black will continue 9...Bxc3 10. bxc3 dxe4 (also good is 10...Nxe4), winning a pawn, for 11. Bxe4 would then lose the Bishop to Black's Knight at f6. One reason for playing 10...dxe4, instead of 10...Nxe4, is that it forces White's d3 Bishop to move, allowing a trade of Queens. This is desirable, for if you are ahead in material, you will want to trade as many pieces as soon as possible, especially the Queen. This will tend to make your material advantage more important while diminishing the significance or possibility of opposing counterattacks.

To reiterate an earlier theme, the possible move 9...Bxc3 emphasizes the idea that one can then attack the center indirectly by removing something that guards it. Once again, it's clear that a dark-square Bishop can influence a light square (A Bishop on b4 can attack the square e4 by capturing on c3).

White has a number of possible defenses here. For one, he could advance his pawn 9. e5, which threatens Black's Knight. But after 9...Ng4, White's safest protection for his advanced pawn is 10. Bf4. That, however, leads to the exchange of the pawn after 10...f6, leaving Black the only pawn in the center (after the exchange), and an open f-file for his Rook. A less good line would be 10. f4, when 10...Bc5+ 11. Kh1 Qh4 is trouble. If then 12. h3, to stop the mate, 12...Qg3 13. hxg4 Qh4 is mate anyway (see diagram 71).

Don't be afraid if it significantly helps your attack without causing too much weakness to move your f-pawns early in the game. Moving the f-pawn may be unwise in the first few moves of the game, when development is crucial. Changing circumstances force principles to be modified in specific situations. Once the King is safely castled, it's sometimes useful to open the f-file for the castled Rook by advancing and exchanging the f-pawn. The Rook can then attack the enemy position, once its own pawn has been traded. It slightly weakens the King's position, but even so it may lead to a powerful attack that outweighs any weakness incurred in its advance. The advance tends to be weak when the diagonal leading to the King can be exploited by a Bishop or a Queen (say, the a2-g8 diagonal, or the a7-g1 diagonal). If it seems that you will be significantly adding to your initiative by advancing the f-pawn, and if the incurred weaknesses seem less important than your attack, then do indeed consider opening the f-file.

White could also add protection to his e-pawn, either by 9. f3, 9. Qf3, or 9. Re1 (diagram 72), but none of these moves seriously annoys Black. In fact, 9. Re1 doesn't quite work.

DIAGRAM 71

DIAGRAM 72

It doesn't work, not so much because it puts the Rook in line to place a pin on the c3 Knight, but because, as in a previous variation, the Knight can be removed. After 9...Bxc3 10. bxc3 dxe4, White can't safely play 11. Bxe4 because of 11....Qxd1 (yes, once again trading Queens—this time to divert the Rook from the Bishop's defense) 12. Rxd1 Nxe4, winning a Bishop. The problem in this variation is that the White Rook was overloaded. It had to guard both d1 and e4 at the same time, so that if it were forced to defend one of those squares, the other one must be abandoned. Avoid overloading pieces. Don't burden a piece with too many responsibilities.

 White plays the most direct defense of all. He captures the pawn, **9. exd5.**

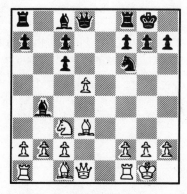

DIAGRAM 73

We've seen that exchanging pawns in this manner means that White has gained time. After Black takes back, it's White who has the next free move. If White had defended instead, then Black would have the *free move* (a move in which one does not have to respond in a particular way). Yes, White's exchange eliminates Black's doubled c-pawns, but they were never a serious drawback anyway. It would be some time before they could be exploited, and right now the initiative seems more significant. Also the move is an answer to Black's threat of winning a pawn.

 Black could play 9...Nxd5, but preferring to rid himself of doubled pawns and to establish power in the center, he plays **9...cxd5.**

DIAGRAM 74

An analysis of the position shows that:
- It is White's move, and he still has the initiative.
- Black has the only pawn in the center, thus a better chance to control the region.
- White will be able to complete his development sooner.
- White's pieces seem to be bearing down on the Black Kingside.

With the initiative, White probably stands slightly better. Yet, if White can't exploit his edge in time and development, Black's center pawn may ultimately give Black the advantage.

On Analysis

Analysis is the process of determining by careful examination the best moves in a variation or position. The ability to analyze is an essential tool in a chessplayer's arsenal. It's also related to the art of problem solving itself, involving two types of reasoning: (1) specific calculation, in which you consider particular moves and variations, evaluating them, weighing their strengths, weaknesses, and consequences; and (2) general judgments, such as what types of moves or plans, rather than what specific ones, you wish to consider.

The real purpose of analysis is this: Until you know precisely where you stand, you cannot decide what your best course of action should be. So first you analyze the situation, then you choose a plan that is consistent with it. In other words, as with any problem-solving situation, you determine what is given, decide what your goal is, then develop a plan of action that seems to bring you to that goal.

To repeat, there are two types of analysis:

• Specific analysis.
• General analysis.

Grandmaster Alexander Kotov, a top Soviet chess teacher for many years, suggests being systematic in your thought processes. When it's your turn, try to find the best move, answering the opponent's threats, maintaining your own, and doing whatever the exigencies of the position require. When it's your opponent's turn, and he's doing the thinking, that's your time to be making general plans, considering the strategy and ideas that might be worth doing if chances should later materialize.

What types of things are considered in a general analysis?
More than the elements to be considered, which we'll soon get into, is the process for eliciting information. You do so by asking probing questions that help you construct a picture of the position, in terms of strengths and weaknesses, possible attacks, piece placements, and so on. This technique, known as the analytic method, is the basis of problem solving and it can be traced back thousands of years to the Greek philosophers and thinkers.

Asking questions can be helpful at any point during the game, whether you're on the move or your opponent is. For example, on your turn, your reasoning might go like this (just after your opponent has played his move):

• Does my opponent's last move threaten me in any way?

If it does, this leads automatically to the next question:
• What can I do about it?

When you have answered this question satisfactorily, you will have found your next move. A more pleasant sort of question to put is:

- Has my opponent responded adequately to the threat contained in my previous move?
- If not, can I now execute my threat to good effect?
- If not, why not?

And so on. You need not ask only these questions, nor do you have to phrase them particularly this way. The questions should direct your attention to what's important. If they're appropriate for the immediate situation, they will more or less suggest the answer. In this sense they serve the same purpose as principles. They do no more and no less than activate and direct the thinking process.

For more general situations, the questions usually dwell on other factors.

- Have I successfully completed my development?
- Does my position contain any weak points?
- If so, what can I do to strengthen them?
- What targets should I be focusing on in my opponent's camp?
- How should I go about assailing them?

Clearly, your questions form a mixture of the specific and the abstract. Usually, the specific pertain to immediate concerns; the abstract, to long-range possibilities and future plans. Both types of questions are useful and necessary in any analysis. You should try to incorporate them into your thinking (or suitable alternatives) at once. This technique takes practice. Use it and eventually you should find yourself improving your overall game play. You'll then find yourself well on the way to mastery of the most challenging and entertaining game ever invented.

The Tenth and Eleventh Moves

 White now continues **10. Bg5.**

DIAGRAM 75

This move pins the Knight, but it's not really the Knight that White has in focus, though, indeed, White might try to pile up on the pinned piece if feasible. The immediate point of White's move is to weaken the Black d-pawn by removing the protection for it. Once again we see that a dark-square Bishop can indirectly attack a light square by threatening to capture the piece that guards that square. One terrible error that Black could now make is 10...Bg4.

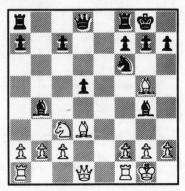

DIAGRAM 76

Black's possible move, 10...Bg4, is potentially quite an annoyance, issuing as it does a direct attack to the White Queen. Moreover, the Bishop is protected by the Knight at f6, so that White cannot win the Bishop by 11. Qxg4 because of 11...Nxg4. But the Bishop's protection is not really so solid. How can White play and win a piece?

White wins a piece by playing a zwischenzug (in-between move). Instead of dealing with the attack to his Queen, he first removes the piece defending the bishop by 11. Bxf6.

At this point, White would be ahead a Knight. His queen is attacked, but so is Black's. If Black were to continue 11...Bxd1, White would answer 12. Bxd8. Neither side has won or lost a

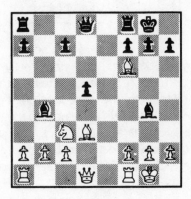

DIAGRAM 77

Queen (they've traded Queens), but White is still ahead a minor piece. Black could then take White's Bishop at d8, but then White takes Black's Bishop at d1. White is then still ahead a minor piece. And if Black answers White's 11. Bxf6 with 11...Qxf6, for example, evening the score temporarily, White merely captures the light-square Bishop with his Queen (12. Qxg4) and escapes with an extra minor piece.

White's zwischenzug illustrates the tactic of removing the defender or removing the guard—undermining. It's these unexpected turns that can make a chess game so interesting.

Black's Many Possibilities

Can't Black simply clarify the position with 10...h6?

DIAGRAM 78

It surely does clear up matters. If White is lucid he will see that 11. Bxf6 wins material. Perhaps Black will play 10...h6, thinking that if White maintains the pin with 11. Bh4, he might be able to break it with 11...g5, driving the Bishop back to g3. This could hold here (if White allowed it to happen), but ordinarily (as well as here), moving the pawns in front of the King's position like this, even to break a pin, can be risky. The defender has to be careful of a possible sacrifice to eliminate the pawns and their coverage of the defending King, as well as merely exploiting the weaknesses these advances engender, even if it takes a few moves. Weaknesses don't vanish by themselves. Once you've committed your pawns to advancing, you're stuck with the consequences.

However, here White doesn't have to retreat his Bishop. He wins material instead with 11. Bxf6.

Black has two responses to this capture. He can take back with his g-pawn (11...gxf6—see diagram 79) or with his Queen (11...Qxf6). The capture 11...gxf6, even if it didn't lose material, looks terrible. Black's Kingside is ripped open totally, and the direct 12. Qh5, simultaneously attacking the h-pawn and the d-pawn (in conjunction with the Knight) appear sufficient to gain an advantage. If 12...Bxc3, a zwischenzug to first remove one of the attackers of the d-pawn, White plays an in-between move of his own, 13. Qxh6, threatening mate.

After that is dealt with, say by 13...f5, White can stop and collect the Bishop at c3. After 12...Bxc3 13. Qxh6, Black could try to clear away some room for his King to escape, but White then mates: 13...Re8 14. Bh7+ (better than 14. Qh7+, which frees the square f8 for Black's King) 14...Kh8 15. Bg6+ (in order to be attacking the f7 square where mate is to take place) 15...Kg8 16. Qh7+ (now is the right time for the Queen to invade) 16...Kf8 17. Qxf7 mate.

DIAGRAM 79

But more direct than 12. Qh5 is the immediate 12. Nxd5!

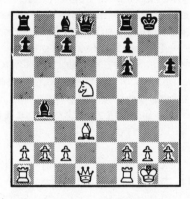

DIAGRAM 80

This captures the d-pawn at once. It also gives an attack to the dark-square Bishop and brings the Knight into position to attack the Black Kingside. Why can't the Knight be captured by the Black Queen (12...Qxd5)?

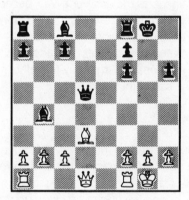

DIAGRAM 81

Look at the alignment of White and Black pieces on the d-file (after 12...Qxd5). If White's Bishop were not on d3, White's Queen could take Black's. White could move his Bishop away first, say to e2, but it would then be Black's move and he now has time to save his Queen. He could move it away, protect it, or trade Queens, ensuring that he gets a Queen's worth of value for it. So the problem with a move like 13. Be2 is that it's too slow. It gives Black a chance to react. What White would like to do here is move his Bishop at d3 with a gain of time. If so, Black would be unable to react by defending his Queen or moving it. There's only one type of move that can, in a sense, freeze the action. That's a check. So, the winning move for White is 13. Bh7 + !. This loses the Bishop to 13...Kxh7, but it gains the move needed so that White can then follow with 14. Qxd5, winning the frozen Queen.

This is another discovered attack, which was defined earlier. To review, the idea is that an attacking line is uncovered by moving away an intervening piece. In some cases, as here, the intervening unit moves with devastating force (such as a check), which prevents the piece that is thus unveiled from extricating itself.

Another lesson to draw from the previous analysis is how the winning idea was discovered, so to speak. White poses himself a problem with a question: How can I get the Bishop out of the way with a gain of time so that I can capture the Queen? The question practically gives the answer away, because only a check (or, in some cases, extremely powerful threats bordering on mate) can accomplish that. There's only one check—case closed. The right question frames the answer. An additional feature is the need to look for relationships, the way friendly and enemy pieces connect along the same lines.

Look for Relationships

One thing you must do to increase your ability to find tactics, and to heighten your awareness of them, is to form the habit of looking for relationships between pieces and squares. You may do this at first by asking leading questions, such as: Are there any enemy pieces on the same lines as my pieces? Are there two or more enemy pieces on the same rank, file, or diagonal? If not, do several of their pieces connect to the same square? Can my Queen move to a square that connects to several enemy units?

Think in terms of schemes and analogies. Notice how certain tactics seem to occur with the same pieces, or under the same type of situations. And when the tactics are not presently in the position, think: Is there some way I can play to set up tactics in the future? Can I do so without giving away my intentions?

Once you've learned an idea, file it away for the next game. Maybe you'll be able to use it again. Even if it's not possible to use it in a particular position, maybe you can play so that the possibility of it occurring is increased.

Nor does 11...Qxf6 save the day for Black either.

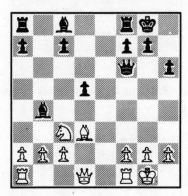

DIAGRAM 82

White simply continues 12. Nxd5, winning a pawn and forking the Queen, the Bishop at b4, and the c-pawn. If Black then tries to reestablish the material balance by 12...Qxb2, capturing a pawn and equally protecting his Bishop, White plays 14. Rb1 (Rooks belong on open files), skewering the Queen and Bishop (diagram 83). After the Queen moves to safety, perhaps to a3, White's Rook or Knight can take Black's Bishop. Once White is a piece ahead, he's set to try a systematic exchange of pieces, reducing counterplay and literally leaving his opponent nothing. the extra piece eventually will decide the outcome. Either it will enable White to develop a winning mating attack, or it will win more material, increasing White's overall advantage. "Material makes material" is the maxim. With a material advantage, it's easier to win more material. Concentrate on using these advantages. Play down your disadvantages. Always play to win. Always.

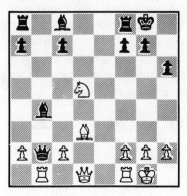

DIAGRAM 83

A logical step for Black is to defend his d-pawn. He could play 10...c6.

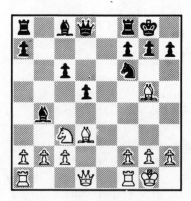

DIAGRAM 84

This is solid defense, ending all immediate threats against the d-pawn. It's only drawbacks are the move doesn't develop a new piece, and in some cases it will lose a tempo if Black should move his pawn to c5 (where, along with the d-pawn, it would control a block of squares along the 4th rank).

Another idea is to defend the d-pawn by 10...Be6. The Bishop move develops a new piece and also adequately secures the d-pawn. Sometimes, though, the Bishop is a better defensive piece at g6, where it cuts the White light-square bishop's d3-h7 diagonal. To get to g6 Black must find the time and safety to play Bg4 and then Bh5 and then Bg6. We've seen that 10...Bg4 loses a piece because of the pin. To retain this possible maneuver of shifting the Bishop to g6, Black now plays **10...Be7,** breaking the pin.

DIAGRAM 85

Now if White plays 11. Qf3, with the idea of clearing the center files for his Rooks (the Queen Rook goes to the d-file and the King Rook to the e-file) and exerting pressure against the d-pawn, Black can follow with 11...Bg4, gaining time to shift back to g6 via h5. Another try for White now is simply 11. Re1, seizing the open file (Rooks need open files). Instead, White goes into a forcing line based on exchanging a Bishop for a Knight. He plays **11. Bxf6.**

DIAGRAM 86

 Since 11...gxf6 makes little sense, other than to accept a busted-up Kingside, Black takes back with his Bishop, **11...Bxf6.**

DIAGRAM 87

III

Endgame: Just a Little

CHAPTER 10

Thinking about the Endgame

White's plan here has been to increase pressure against the only pawn in the center, the Black d-pawn. Consistent with this is 12. Qh5, threatening both mate and the target pawn (d5).

DIAGRAM 88

If Black defends with 12...g6, play might continue 13. Qxd5. After 13...Qxd5 14. Nxd5 Bxb2 15. Ra-b1 Be5 (to protect the c-pawn) 16. Rf-e1 Bd6 17. Nf6+ Kh8 (17...Kg7 allows 18. Ne8+ Kg8 19. Nxd6 cxd6 20. Be4, winning at least the exchange—a rook for a minor piece) 18. Be4, and Black must lose an exchange. Of course, to avoid the weakening of the f6 square Black could have played 12...h6 instead. Moreover, he doesn't have to play

14...Bxb2, opening the b-file for White's Rook and leading to some of the tactical problems of the above variation. And after 13. Qxd5, Black can assure reaching an endgame a pawn down after 13...Bxc3 (removing the defender of the Queen) 14. Qxd8 (a zwischenzug, saving the Queen before recapturing on c3) Rxd8, when White's extra doubled c-pawn may not be sufficient to win. Very often, an extra pawn is sufficient to win, but probably not here. It depends on its value in the ensuing endgame.

How is it that an extra pawn usually wins, and how is the win executed?

Having an extra pawn doesn't mean very much in the opening, when time, development, and the initiative supersede. An extra pawn stars in the endgame, when it has a real chance to forge ahead and become a new Queen. The theory of the endgame actually derives from the conversion of an extra pawn into a win. The pawn itself may so move to become a new Queen, and with that additional force, checkmate can't be too far away. Or the advancing pawn may force the losing side to sacrifice more material to stop it, probably a Knight or Bishop. With the extra piece it has won for its pawn, the superior side will probably be able to win additional pawns, which also may threaten to Queen. Sooner or later, the superior side will either force mate or increase its material advantage so greatly that mate becomes imminent.

The winning technique is fairly direct. The stronger side should systematically try to exchange pieces, minor piece for minor piece, Rook for Rook, and Queen for Queen. He must be chary about trading pawns, however, for if he swaps too many, the inferior side may see his chance to give up a minor piece for the final pawn. With no pawns left, it's impossible to make a new Queen. Meanwhile, the extra minor piece itself, without the presence of pawns, may not lead to a forced win.

A further benefit of systematic exchanges is that they virtually reduce all counterplay. One generally needs material to create attacking chances, and the less you have, the easier it becomes to defend. And, the extra pawn becomes more important as well.

This is summed up in the principle:

• Exchange when ahead.

The corollary is:

• Avoid exchanges when behind.

More on the Endgame

Of the three phases, the endgame is the least understood and worst played. Indeed, the mark of a really strong player is the ability to convert endgame advantages consistently into victories.

Endgames can vary tremendously, but they tend to have a number of common characteristics:

1) Usually, less material is on the board and the Queen is gone.

2) Advantages in pieces and pawns in the endgame tend to be decisive, whereas in the opening and middlegame material superiority can be countered by other factors, such as the initiative and King safety.

3) Pawns in the endgame assume greater importance because they may threaten to become new Queens by reaching the 8th rank.

4) Perhaps the most distinctive feature of the endgame is that, unlike the opening or the middlegame, the King can be active without fear of stumbling into a sudden mate. There generally aren't enough enemy men left to pose serious threats.

Many endgames actually resolve into situations of King and pawns against King and pawns. Then victory may hinge on the ability of one King to outmaneuver its opposing counterpart. The principle is:

• The King can be a strong piece. Use it.

To return to our game:
White instead plays **12. Nxd5** (diagram 89), perceiving that
12...Qxd5 again loses the Queen to a discovery (13. Bxh7 +).

DIAGRAM 89

Black could accept that he's dropped a pawn, completing his
development, say by 12...Be6. Then after 13. Nxf6 + Qxf6, his
chances of achieving a draw in the pawn-down endgame would
not be very good.

So he snatches back his pawn, **12...Bxb2.** With only one safe
square for White's attacked Rook, he plays **13. Rb1,** menacing
the Bishop. And Black is still unable to safely capture the Knight
at d5 because of the discovery Bxh7 + .

DIAGRAM 90

We question: Where should Black move his attacked Bishop? The c3 square is guarded by the Knight, though he could retreat it all the way back to f6. The move 13...Bd4 (diagram 91) fails to another discovery, 14. Bxh7 + (diagram 92) Kxh7 15. Qxd4.

DIAGRAM 91

DIAGRAM 92

It may seem that Black, with 15...c6, can attack White's Knight pinned to its Queen by the Black Queen. But White can get his Queen out of the pin with a gain of time by 16. Qd3 + . After Black gets out of check, White can move his Knight to safety.

The defense 13...Be5 (diagram 93) also flops, a simple winning line being 14. Bxh7 + ! Kxh7 15. Qh5 + (diagram 94) forking both the King and the Bishop at e5) Kg8 16. Qxe5. Black could then try 16...Re8, bringing the Rook to an open file with a gain of time while attacking White's Queen. But White has the escape 17. Qh5, still keeping his Knight protected. The further annoyance 17...g6 doesn't disrupt the Knight's defense either, for White still has 18. Qf3, when the Queen is free of Black threats and the Knight is upheld.

Another possibility for Black is to move the Bishop slightly out of play with 13...Ba3. Here the Bishop doesn't contribute to the Kingside defense, and may fall victim to an insidious veiled threat

DIAGRAM 93

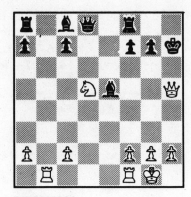

DIAGRAM 94

if White plays a timely Qf3. In the right circumstances, if the White Queen moves to f3 it would menace two potential discoveries: the Black Bishop at a3 by moving the Bishop at d3; and the Black Rook at a8 by shifting the Knight at d5. Remember to look for possible tactics by noting which pieces line up on the same rank, file, or diagonal.

Grappling for Advantage

 Black elects to play **13...Bf6.**

DIAGRAM 95

If we scan the position here we notice several things:

- White is much better developed.
- Black must yet develop his Queen Bishop.
- White's Rook occupies the open b-file.
- Black's Queen Rook doesn't yet have a safe move, thanks to White controlling the b-file.
- As long as White's Knight can occupy d5 without fear of capture it imposes severe threats on Black.
- White has the move and a decent initiative.

White now has several interesting moves, such as 14. Qf3, threatening a discovery on the a8-Rook as well as smashing up Black's Kingside by 15. Nxf6+; or 14. Be4, threatening to win the exchange via 15. Nxf6+ and 16. Bxa8; or 14. Qh5, once again threatening mate and attempting to force weakening pawn moves on the Black Kingside.

White indeed essays **14. Qh5.**

DIAGRAM 96

Safest for Black is 14...h6, so that his Bishop is still protected by the g-pawn.

Perhaps because it seems to gain time while driving away the White Queen, Black tries **14...g6** (diagram 97). This attacks the Queen but unfortunately creates immediate weaknesses at h6 and f6, the last leaving the Bishop not as well protected. A winning tactic is now launched by **15. Qf3** (diagram 98). This threatens the Bishop at f6 immediately, also putting the Queen in line to issue a discovered attack to the Rook at a8 by moving the Knight.

Black seems to have two choices: he can defend the bishop with his King, 15...Kg7, or get it to safety by repositioning the attacked Bishop (15...Bg7). Getting the Bishop out of attack would generally be the more reliable defense, for it's not yet time to use the King unless it were the only way to save the Bishop. So Black continued **15...Bg7** (diagram 99), which also restores

DIAGRAM 97

DIAGRAM 98

DIAGRAM 99

control over the two previously weakened squares, f6 and h6. As a rule, a piece doesn't guard the square it occupies. Nor does it guard itself. Move it away and then it guards the square it used to be on.

White now has the chance for a discovery to the Rook at a8 by moving his Knight, but where?

If the Knight is moved to e3 or f4, for example, Black cannot save the Rook by moving it, for b8 is guarded by White's well-placed Rook, currently dominating the open b-file. Black can nonetheless save the Rook by moving his light-square Bishop (finally), so that the Queen then defends the Rook. The real question is which discovery is the most effective? Can Black move the Knight with a gain of time? That is, can it be moved to pose an additional threat to the Rook now attacked by the Queen? White would then have two threats, and Black might be unable to guard against both. One winner is 16. Nf6+, which forces Black to save his King. After he does so, say by 16..Qxf6, developing a new piece, White can go ahead with his other threat and capture the Rook with 17. Qxa8.

Another idea for White is to move the Knight and capture something in the process, even if it leaves the Knight in a position to be captured. If Black takes the Knight, he still loses the Rook and whatever the Knight captured in the first place. White decides to try **16. Nxc7** (diagram 100) snaring a pawn and issuing a double attack to the Rook. Now even if Black's Bishop cleared off the back row, the Knight could still take the Rook.

DIAGRAM 100

One defensive idea is to clear the back rank with a gain of time. If the Bishop at c8 could menacingly enter the play, maybe the Rook could use the time to save itself. Now 16...Qxc7 would win the Knight but drop the Rook to 17. Qxa8. But Black reasons that **16...Bg4** (diagram 101) is plausible. His analysis went 17. Qxg4 Qxc7. But he overlooks one thing—that the Rook at a8 is doubly attacked.

DIAGRAM 101

White answers **16...Bg4,** not by capturing the Bishop, but by taking the Rook at a8 with his Queen—it being protected by the Knight. White's move: **17. Qxa8.**

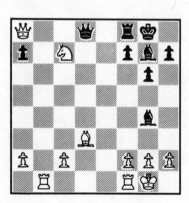

DIAGRAM 102

Black really now has two choices: he can take White's Knight, uncovering an attack on White's Queen from his Rook in the process, or he can take the Queen with his own, knowing he will still be able to capture the Knight a move later. He makes the less wise choice and captures the Queen: **17...Qxa8.**

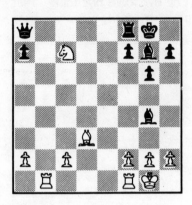

DIAGRAM 103

CHAPTER

12

The Final Phase: Forcing Exchanges

There are two ways to play defense. You can play passively, taking no chances and, like most beginners, trying to guard everything or trading down to avoid attacks against you. Or, like most experienced players, you can play actively, combining defense with counterattack, as exemplified in the play of the Soviet School. The latter is riskier but more apt to succeed. Just think of the adage "the best defense is a good offense." Black's best course of action was to play 17...Qxc7, retaining his Queen so as to be able to launch counterattacks. **17...Qxa8** leads into a cut-and-dried endgame which is quite safe but also quite hopeless.

It's a poor choice because, when behind in material, one should try to avoid exchanges, especially of Queens. Such transactions only kill counterplay and steer the game closer to a situation where additional material assumes greater importance. White and Black now are virtually forced to respond. White has to retake the Queen **18. Nxa8** (diagram 104) and Black must pick up the Knight (before it runs away) by **18...Rxa8** (diagram 105).

Let's once again evaluate the position. Black has four pawns, while White has five. White so far in our calculation is ahead by a pawn. Not counting the Kings, both sides have three pieces, but White has two Rooks and a Bishop whereas Black has two Bishops and a Rook. Since one Rook and Bishop balance out for each side, the difference is that Black has a Bishop for a Rook. Take into account White's extra pawn, and the exact equation

DIAGRAM 104

DIAGRAM 105

reads: White has a Rook and a pawn for a Bishop. It's White's move, and he's got to form a plan.

Always Play With a Plan

Chess is, above all, a logical game. Things happen on the board as they are made to happen. Organization and consistency are almost always rewarded. It may be difficult at first, but you must strive in every game to form a series of feasible plans and to implement them faithfully and economically. Often a bad plan is better than no plan at all. If you form a bad plan, and lose because of it, you can review afterward on where you went wrong and on how to improve next time. If you've played without a plan, there will be little to learn from your defeat.

Your plan at any point in the game needn't be elaborate. It could be something as basic as determining how best to complete your development, or on which side to castle and why, or whether to attack now or prepare your assault further by improving the position of one or more of your pieces. But always have an objective in mind and make your play conform to it as far as conditions on the board allow.

Beginners may tend to play aimlessly, jumping from one idea to the next without reason. On the other hand, more experienced players sometimes err in the other direction. They choose a plan and then follow it blindly, no matter where it may lead. The ideal is to plan ahead but to be flexible at the same time: You might have to change a plan. After all, if your planned objective is to win a pawn and your opponent puts his Queen where you can take it for nothing, you will usually do well to abandon your original goal (at least temporarily) and snatch the Queen instead.

• Don't be afraid to change your mind if you see a better idea or suddenly realize that you are about to make a mistake. At the same time, be sure your reason for changing is legitimate.

You needn't strive to look very far ahead at first, a move or two will usually suffice. Often it's not possible to see far along anyway. Calculation—working out precise moves and their sequences—should be an aid to planning and not an end in itself. It's easier to spot good moves when you have a clear notion what you are looking for.

Planning falls under the heading of strategy. Carrying out one's plans involves tactics. The two are related but different.

What's the difference between strategy and tactics?

These two terms are virtual opposites, but they are also counterparts, which is why chessplayers may confuse them. A further complication arises in that they have an everyday usage outside of chess, where the meanings are even more distorted.

Strategy concerns an overall plan. It's usually long-term and of a general nature. A strategy may consist of an attack on the Kingside, for example. It may comprise a number of maneuvers (a series of quiet or uncontested moves aimed at a specific goal, or a repositioning of a particular piece) and accompanying moves. For longer affairs, three or four strategies per side are not uncommon. Sometimes a strategy is confined to a particular phase (the opening, middlegame, or endgame), and sometimes it overlaps from one phase to the other. Less often, a specific strategy may dominate throughout an entire game. But strategies can go with the wind and a player must adapt to the vicissitudes of move-to-move combat. Most often, strategy and planning are synonymous.

Tactics are a different story. They are the individual operations needed to execute a strategy. They tend to be short-term and immediate, specific and concrete. If strategy is what you plan to do, tactics are specifically how you'll do it.

Since tactical operations make up practically all of the game, it's easier to study them because of their sheer preponderance. You get lots of opportunities to seek out forks, pins, and skewers. But strategy is less numerous, requiring the ability to see an overview (something usually taking experience and time), and is much harder to learn. For this reason newcomers tend to learn tactics rather early on.

This brings me back to the argument that in chess, before you can see the whole, it helps to understand the individual parts first. Know what goes into a strategy and the strategy itself fits together.

Back to Our Game

The correct strategy when ahead in material is to trade off pieces, accentuating your advantage, for it's harder for the enemy to offset your extra force. It's also important to take note of what the difference in force here really constitutes.

In addition to his extra pawn, White has a Rook for a Bishop. To win a Rook for a Bishop or Knight is to "win the exchange." This is advantageous because in direct matchups a Rook can generally contain either Bishop or Knight without diminishing its own power. A Rook is also a mating threat whereas solo Bishops and Knights usually are not.

The correct plan for playing with this advantage was outlined by Capablanca. Use your greater mobility to attack and force your opponent to play defensively. Keep up the pressure, eke out as much as you can from the position, and at the right moment, sacrifice your Rook for the minor piece, simplifying to a winning endgame. The trade-down usually works if in the process you win a pawn, which can then be made into a new Queen.

Here, White is already up a pawn, so his task is considerably eased. To best feel the effects of being up the exchange, it would make sense to exchange a pair of rooks, leaving Black only his Bishops. White's remaining Rook would then have no counterbalancing force.

In helping a student form a game plan, so that he can do it on his own in the future, I will ask a number of leading questions that more or less take the following form:

• Does Black have any potential targets?
• If so, does White have his pieces on the best squares to flail away at those targets?
• Does Black have a satisfactory way to defend those points?
• Can White force the exchange of a pair of Rooks?
• If so, would that increase his winning chances in this position?
• Are there any general rules that apply here or that might supply some guidance?
• Can White play flexibly, so that he manages to achieve a number of simultaneous aims?

These are only sample questions, but they indicate the kind of reasoning process alluded to earlier. The questions need not be asked in this order, nor do they have to be framed exactly in this manner. However and whatever questions you pose, the aim is to make them serve you in the thinking process so that you are able to choose an intelligent, logical course of action.

Does White have any potential targets for attack?

Other than the possibility of driving away his light-square Bishop by a move like h3, the two points that White can zero in on are f7 and a7. How can White attack those points? He can hit the a-pawn only with his Rooks, which he can do from along the a-file, the 7th rank, or a combination of both. The f-pawn can be attacked by both Rooks along the 7th rank. The f7 square can also be approached by White's Bishop along the a2-f7 diagonal (from c4). Black can defend the a-pawn with his Rook (as long as it's not driven away (say by Be4) or traded off, and by the dark-square Bishop from d4. The f-pawn can be guarded by the King, the Rook from f8 and the Bishop from e6. So it seems that defenses are so far adequate, but it may be possible to combine attacking moves from both plans into one scheme.

Can White trade off a pair of Rooks? It's pretty clear that he can. All he has to do is to double his Rooks on the b-file and then move the front one up to b8, where it's protected by the back one. (More on this plan shortly.) With White then having the only Rook, he will be able to attack more freely without having to cope with Black's most important defender.

Are there any general guidelines to consider?

A number come to mind with regard to the Rooks. White already has a Rook on the open b-file, uncontested, which means that White controls the b-file. After occupying an open file, the next thing a Rook should endeavor to do is to reach its 7th rank. From there, it often remains in position to attack an entire row of enemy pieces and pawns. Meanwhile, it's also admirably placed to deliver mating threats. Sometimes, in order to dominate an open line, one has to double Rooks, which strictly speaking is not necessary here.

Doubled Rooks refers to a situation in which a player's Rooks line up on the same row. Whether in attack or defense, on a rank or file, such a battery presents the possessor with rich tactical possibilities. The most awesome stratagems occur when two Rooks occupy the 7th rank. So part of White's plan here might be to get both Rooks to the 7th rank. From there, they can wreak havoc, attacking both of Black's target squares.

The secret here is to play flexibly, so that White can somehow achieve all ends of the plan, or at least to retain all the options. He would like to:

- Attack both f7 and a7.
- Occupy the 7th rank with both Rooks.
- Double on the b-file to force a trade of Rooks.

White therefore plays 19. Rb7.

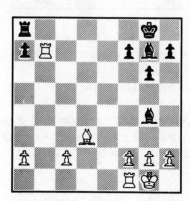

DIAGRAM 106

White has established a beachhead with this incursion into the heart of the Black terrain. He now is presenting Black with several serious threats. To double on the b-file, preparing to exchange Rooks, is one. Another is to attack f7 again with 20. Bc4, which only results in further trades after 20...Be6 21. Bxe6 fxe6. If the light-square Bishops are then exchanged, the 7th rank would become even more exposed and vulnerable. In anticipation of White's bishop redeployment, Black plays **19...Be6** (diagram 107).

This defends the f-pawn and also prevents White's Bishop from assuming a commanding post at c4. Moreover, it seems to counterattack by targeting the White a-pawn. White could save this pawn by moving it out of attack, but that would cost him time. If he's going to execute his plan efficiently, he really shouldn't be making unnecessary pawn moves. For reasons that

DIAGRAM 107

will soon become clear, the a-pawn is immune. To take it would leave Black open to a trap.

If you are lured into a line of play that seems to be good but really isn't, you have fallen for a *trap*. The most familiar traps occur in the opening when unsuspecting opponents capture easily attained material. The present situation no longer involves the opening, but there's a booby-trap waiting for Black, so he'd better step carefully.

 White continues with his plan (don't veer from your plan unless you must or see a new opportunity) and plays **20. Rf-b1,** doubling Rooks.

DIAGRAM 108

If Black wanted to, he could now avoid an immediate trade of Rooks by playing a move like 20...Rf8. If White were then to continue 21. Rb8, as per his plan, Black could interpose his Bishop at c8. Naturally, this wouldn't delay matters for very long, because White might be able to then double Rooks on the 8th rank, or if necessary use the open King or Queen files to penetrate the Black position. Sooner or later, Black would have to make further concessions, or lose more material, or a combination of both. The end result would be the same, he would lose, but only if White were to find strong moves. You will assume, of course, that your opponent is capable of finding the best moves, but you must actually make him prove that he can do it. Top Russian players, in particular, will fight like the devil to retrieve hopeless positions. World champion Anatoly Karpov, for example, in the final stages of his first match of 1984-85 with challenger Gary Kasparov, played on in a hopeless position hoping for a stalemate. Make it hard for your opponent, and you might be rewarded. Russian world champion Alexander Alekhine once said that to capture the victory from him you had to beat him three times: "once in the opening, once in the middlegame, and once in the endgame." He never gave up without a fight.

Perhaps the final word on this should be that of grandmaster Saviely Tartakover (1887-1956). The Russian-born writer and teacher once said: "No one ever won a game by resigning."

As fruitless as it might seem, Black might be able to improve his chances if he can get away with avoiding a trade of Rooks.

Black plays 20...Bxa2, gobbling the offering.

DIAGRAM 109

The capture also attacks White's Rook at b1, but White will have the time to cope with this threat after first checking on the back rank, to force an exchange of Rooks. White plays **21. Rb8+.**

DIAGRAM 110

Black could try 21...Bf8 here, instead of taking White's Rook, thinking that if he loses his Rook at a8 he'll still be able to capture White's Rook at b1. But after 22. Rxa8 Bxb1 23. Rxa7 (threatening 24. Ra1 garnering the Bishop) 23...Bg7 (to guard a1)

24.Ra8+ (to force the Bishop back, off the a1-h8 diagonal) 24...Bf8 25. Ra1, White wins the Bishop after all. So Black simply trades Rooks, **21...Rxb8** (Diagram 111). White takes back **22. Rxb8+** (Diagram 112). Black, having only one legal move, is forced to play **22...Bf8** (Diagram 113).

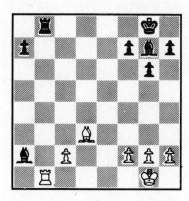

DIAGRAM 111

DIAGRAM 112

DIAGRAM 113

The position now poses a final problem. White is still up the exchange, but he lost back his extra pawn when Black's light-square Bishop captured on a2. The difficulty with so many captures like Bxa2 is they often lead to the Bishop being trapped (a famous instance being the first game of the Fischer-Spassky match in 1972, when Bobby couldn't extricate his cornered Bishop satisfactorily). Here, the Bishop is not yet trapped because it can retreat if attacked (say by 23. Rb2) along the a2-e6 diagonal. This suggests a solution to the problem: How to close the diagonal, to make it impossible for the Bishop to retreat. One move in particular materializes, that of **23. c4!**

DIAGRAM 114

There is now no way that Black can extricate his Bishop safely. White will capture it in two moves, beginning with 24. Rb2. See how the well-placed Rook currently prevents the dark-square Bishop from assisting in a possible defense of the key b2 square by pinning the Bishop to the King. Ahead a whole Rook after this, White will have little trouble bringing home victory.

Here I stopped the game, but in an actual game Black would probably resign anyway. Being up an extra Rook almost always insures victory. If you haven't yet learned how to win with an extra Rook, however, you might want to continue playing just to see how it's done. The general technique for exchanging down has been outlined earlier.

Appendix

A Few Suggestions

1. Play the board, not the person. Assume your opponent makes the best moves. Reason out all moves, your opponent's as well as your own.
2. Play to control, occupy, and influence the center of the board.
3. Develop all pieces quickly to effective squares, moving each piece just once. Try to mount multiple attacks.
4. Move both center pawns, preferably two squares each. Don't make unnecessary pawn moves.
5. Develop your minor pieces first, then your Queen and Rooks.
6. Castle early for defense and attack.
7. Don't waste time or moves. Don't go pawn grabbing. Don't give pointless threats, such as isolated checks.
8. Place your Rooks on open or half-open files or on lines likely to clear. Then double your Rooks and invade to the 7th and 8th ranks.
9. Play flexibly, but always with a plan. Try to look several moves ahead to foresee enemy attacks and defenses.
10. Concentrate. Utilize principles and other guidelines, but never lose sight of the position before you. Most moves should be supported by specific as well as general logic.

The Moves of the Game

1.	e4	e5
2.	Nf3	Nc6
3.	d4	exd4
4.	Nxd4	Nf6
5.	Nc3	Bb4
6.	Nxc6	bxc6
7.	Bd3	0-0
8.	0-0	d5
9.	exd5	cxd5
10.	Bg5	Be7
11.	Bxf6	Bxf6
12.	Nxd5	Bxb2
13.	Rb1	Bf6
14.	Qh5	g6
15.	Qf3	Bg7
16.	Nxc7	Bg4
17.	Qxa8	Qxa8
18.	Nxa8	Rxa8
19.	Rb7	Be6
20.	Rf-b1	Bxa2
21.	Rb8+	Rxb8
22.	Rxb8+	Bf8
23.	c4	Black resigns

(1–0)

Index

About the Author

Bruce Pandolfini, a U.S. National Chess Master, gained prominence as an analyst on PBS's live telecast of the Fischer-Spassky championship match in 1972. In due course, he lectured widely on chess and in 1978 was chosen to deliver the Bobby Fischer Chess Lectures at the University of Alabama in Birmingham. His first book, *Let's Play Chess,* appeared in 1980. The author is a *Chess Life* magazine consulting editor, for which he writes the monthly "ABC's of Chess." He is the author of *Bobby Fischer's Outrageous Chess Moves* and *One Move Chess by the Champions* and has also written columns for *Time-Video,* the *Litchfield County Times,* and *Physician's Travel and Meeting Guide.*

As a chess teacher, he's been on the faculty of the New School for Social Research since 1973, and currently conducts chess classes at Browning, Trinity, and the Little Red School House in New York City. With U.S. Champion Lev Alburt, he has developed special children's programs sponsored by the American Chess Foundation. The director of the world famous Manhattan Chess Club at Carnegie Hall, Pandolfini visited the USSR in the fall of 1984 to study their teaching methods and observe the controversial championship match between Anatoly Karpov and Gary Kasparov.

FIRESIDE CHESS LIBRARY

Just a reminder about the treasure of chess books from Fireside, for all players from beginners to advanced chess masters!

New titles:

ONE MOVE CHESS BY THE CHAMPIONS
Bruce Pandolfini
128 pgs, 60608-5, $6.95

BOBBY FISCHER'S OUTRAGEOUS CHESS MOVES
Bruce Pandolfini
128 pgs, 60609-3, $6.95

PRINCIPLES OF THE NEW CHESS
Bruce Pandolfini
144 pgs, 60719-7, $6.95 (Available March '86)

Chess backlist:

CHESS FOR BEGINNERS
I.A. Horowitz
134 pgs, 21184-6, $5.95

CHESS OPENINGS
I.A. Horowitz
792 pgs, 20553-6, $16.95

CHESS TRAPS
I.A. Horowtiz & Fred Reinfeld
250 pgs, 21041-6, $6.95

HOW TO THINK AHEAD IN CHESS
I.A. Horowitz & Fred Reinfeld
274 pgs, 21138-2, $6.95

THE CHESS COMPANION
Irving Chernev
288 pgs, 21651-1, $9.95

CHESS THE EASY WAY
Reuben Fine
186 pgs, 0-346-12323-2, $5.95

THE MOST INSTRUCTIVE GAMES OF CHESS EVER PLAYED
Irving Chernev
286 pgs, 21536-1, $8.95

CHESS IS AN EASY GAME
Fred Reinfeld
96 pgs, 0-346-12332-1, $2.95

AN INVITATION TO CHESS
Irving Chernev & Kenneth Harkness
224 pgs, 21270-2, $5.95

LOGICAL CHESS, MOVE BY MOVE
Irving Chernev
250 pgs, 21135-8, $7.95

WINNING CHESS
Irving Chernev & Fred Reinfeld
236 pgs, 21114-5, $7.95

HOW TO WIN IN THE CHESS OPENINGS
I.A. Horowitz
192 pgs, 0-346-12445-X, $5.95

CHESS CATECHISM
Larry Evans
256 pgs, 21531-0, $6.95

THE 1,000 BEST SHORT GAMES OF CHESS
Irving Chernev
562 pgs, 53801-2, $7.95

THE FIRESIDE BOOK OF CHESS
Irving Chernev & Fred Reinfeld
406 pgs, 21221-4, $8.95

WINNING CHESS TACTICS ILLUSTRATED
I.A. Horowitz
96 pgs, 0-346-12405-0, $3.95

Send order to:
Simon & Schuster Inc. Dept. CB
1230 Avenue of the Americas
New York, NY 10020

Total costs all books ordered _____
Postage and handling ___$1.50___
New York residents add applicable sales tax _____
Enclosed is my payment for books ordered _____
(check or money order ONLY)

Ship to:
Name _____

Address _____

City _____ State _____ Zip code _____